COOK GAME

COOK GAME

J. C. Jeremy Hobson and Philip Watts

Food and recipe photography by Philip Watts

THE CROWOOD PRESS

First published in 2008 by
The Crowood Press Ltd
Ramsbury, Marlborough
Wiltshire SN8 2HR

www.crowood.com

British Library Cataloguing-in-Publication Data
A catalogue record for this book is available from the British Library.

ISBN 978 1 84797 031 2

Photography Acknowledgements
Unless otherwise indicated, the photographs in this book were taken by Philip Watts and are his copyright. The authors and publishers are grateful to Greg Knight (www.ruralshots.com) for providing additional photographs.

Typeset by Jean Cussons Typesetting, Diss, Norfolk

Printed and bound in Singapore by Craft Print International Ltd

Contents

Dedication

With much love to Melinda and Tricia –
Our own particular favourite 'game birds'!

Acknowledgements

Firstly, special thanks to Philip Watts for all of his photos, help and, most importantly, friendship. Philip has taken all photos with the exception of those on page 41, 47, 95, 157 and 183, which were supplied by Greg Knight of 'Ruralshots' photography (visit his website at www.ruralshots.com) – I am most grateful. The photographs on pages 80, 193, 196 and 201 were taken by Melinda Hobson.

So many kind people have supplied one or more recipes for this book. Others have been very helpful in my making contacts; amongst them: David Venner, Sophie Walker, Neil Penilington, Paul Stark, Eric and Sandra Compton, Susan Willer and Laura Dawson. Valerie Bentley graciously allowed us to photograph a sausage-making session – despite our ribald comments!

Very grateful acknowledgements to Tricia Watts, who, over a period of several days, allowed me unlimited access to her kitchen during the making and testing of some recipes – she was kind enough to say that I'd left the place in a better state than I found it, but somehow I doubt it!

Thanks too, to the various publishing houses that have been good enough to give permission to quote the short pieces at the beginning of each chapter. Namely: Weidenfeld & Nicolson, a division of the Orion Publishing Group, for the extract from *Ermine Tales* by the Earl of Carnarvon; Jonathon Young, editor-in-chief, *The Field*, for permission to quote from *The Changing Year* on page 40. The quote from *Border Reflections* (© Lord Home, 1979), is reprinted by permission of Harper-Collins Publishers Ltd, and those on pages 24 and 122 are reprinted thanks to the kindness of Faber and Faber. Every effort has been made to obtain copyright permission for the extracts that appear at the beginning of Chapters 1 and 10, but as yet, no reply has been forthcoming (the authors would be pleased to hear from anyone in connection with this matter in order that the situation can be rectified in future editions). The remainder are either out of copyright or the copyright is owned by Hobson-Hall Publications. The author and the publisher would like to thank Clarissa Dickson Wright and Kyle Cathie publishers for granting them permission to reproduce the recipe entitled 'Grilled partridge with garlic, oil, lemon and cayenne', which was originally published in *The Game Cookbook* by Clarissa Dickson Wright and Johnny Scott (Kyle Cathie, 2004).

Di Murray of Kezie Foods, based in Berwickshire, was kind enough to give permission to use some of their website facts appertaining to crocodile and kangaroo meat; her help is specifically acknowledged and gratefully received. Paul Crook, the managing director at Osgrow of Bristol, is keen to promote the health benefits of kangaroo and ostrich meat and, as a result, was very forthcoming in his help and in granting permission to reproduce two of their recipes for kangaroo meat. Thanks to Dan Wynde for the 'backwoodsman' recipes, and to Maurice Chemineau, Beatrice Clemensau and Sarah Duval for those with an obvious French flavour. Spanish- and Italian-based recipes were collected and adapted by Philip Watts from an eclectic mix of people, to all of whom we are indebted. Traditional British game recipes were offered by all manner of field sports enthusiasts who were happy to share their family formulas without wishing for specific acknowledgements – however, two we would like to name are Alan and Helen Cooper. Other individuals and organizations have been mentioned in the text.

Particular and effusive thanks for submitting recipes and comments must go to Martyn Nail, executive chef at Claridges; Bryan Ferry; Tony Jacques, aka 'Jack Hughes' of *Countryman's Weekly*; Duff Hart-Davis; Émilie Courtat and Thierry Lacour; Jacques at Chez Jacques; Jane Robins; Sarah Kennedy at the Sun Inn, Helpin, West Yorkshire; the Count Von Baden, Antonio Gamba and Chris Tarrant – without you all, there could have been no 'Special Guest Recipes'.

Finally, I should very much like to express my most sincere appreciation to all those involved at The Crowood Press for their friendship, encouragement and efficiency – it is a pleasure to work *with* a team of real people rather than merely *for* a publishing house.

NOTES AND MEASUREMENTS

Some recipes may have a French, Spanish or Italian influence, but all contain types of fish and game that can be readily sourced in the UK. Some of the more unusual, such as those found in Chapter 13, for example, might not be on the meat and fish counter of your average supermarket, but all are available. Where applicable, some recipes will show how to utilize the less attractive parts of a meat carcass. 'Off-cuts' can be used as a basis for burgers, sausages and stuffing.

I have a hatred of 'new-fangled' kitchen gadgets, but there are times where a food processor, for example, may make life easier and I have mentioned their use in the appropriate places. Otherwise, I prefer using knives to chop and fingers to rub!

All the recipes have been tried and tested – but not necessarily 'in house'. Conversions from Imperial to Metric are not always straightforward – use either one or the other.

Weights and Measures

The author is not great believer in precision cooking, much preferring to belong to the 'add a bit until it tastes right' school of thought! Nevertheless, where it was deemed necessary to be a little more meticulous, the equivalents given below were used.

Some recipes sourced elsewhere may give a slightly different conversion. For example, some give 2oz as being 50g, whereas the majority seem to agree that 55g is the equivalent to 2oz – I have tried to be consistent.

I have also made a point of including the words 'tablespoon' and 'teaspoon' in full, as there can be some confusion when abbreviations are used – a teaspoon of salt may enhance the flavours of a soup or casserole, whereas a tablespoon would not!

Temperature

110°C	225°F	reg. ¼
120°C	250°F	reg. ½
140°C	275°F	reg. 1
150°C	300°F	reg. 2
160°C	325°F	reg. 3
180°C	350°F	reg. 4
190°C	375°F	reg. 5
200°C	400°F	reg. 6
220°C	425°F	reg. 7
230°C	450°F	reg. 8
240°C	475°F	reg. 9

Volume

115ml	4fl oz	140ml	5fl oz
170ml	6fl oz	200ml	7fl oz
280ml	½pt	425ml	¾pt
570ml	1pt	850ml	1½pt
1.1ltr	2pt	1.4ltr	2½pt
1.7ltr	3pt	2.25ltr	4pt

Weight

15g	½oz	30g	1oz
45g	1½oz	55g	2oz
70g	2½oz	85g	3oz
115g	4oz	140g	5oz
170g	6oz	200g	7oz
225g	8oz	285g	10oz
340g	12oz	400g	14oz
450g	1lb	680g	1½lb
900g	2lb	1.35kg	3lb

Introduction

He will bring his nightcap with him, for where the M.F.H. dines he sleeps,
and where the M.F.H. sleeps he breakfasts.

(R.S. Surtees, *Mr Facey Romford's Hounds*, 1865)

Not all that long ago, game dishes were considered 'posh' food; something of a treat to be had when eating out at a restaurant, and game itself was only seasonally seen in the best butchers and never found in the supermarket. Those involved in field sports were, of course, more fortunate in their supply but, even so, if you were in a small pheasant shoot in the south, it was virtually impossible to get your hands on a grouse shot on the moors of Scotland. Country people may have been offered the odd brace of partridge or pheasant as a result of beating on the local shoot, ferreters may have had a regular supply of rabbits, and the deer-stalker a plethora of venison at the right time of year, but for the rest of the population, not only was a supply of game hard to come by, when you could get it, it came complete with a certain aura and mystery, not the least of which was how to prepare and cook it.

The classic methods of cooking game were generally not very imaginative: roast, roast or roast seemed to be the order of the day, and whilst such simple methods undoubtedly make for a wonderful meal, especially when accompanied by game chips and fresh garden vegetables, the majority of people's tastes today are far more eclectic. No wonder then, that with ever-increasing availability of game and fish – nowadays made possible through the willingness of supermarkets to stock it, and the public's awareness that it makes a good, healthy meal, low in cholesterol and high in protein – there is a need to think 'out of the box' when it comes to creating different recipes for what is rapidly becoming 'everyday' food.

The popularity of game is due in no small part to the championing of its cause by 'celebrity' chefs such as Clarissa Dickson Wright, Rick Stein, Marco-Pierre White and Hugh Fearnley-Whittingstall, and to the 'Game's On' and 'Game to Eat' campaigns, spear-headed by the British Association for Shooting and Conservation (BASC) and the Countryside Alliance. More power to their respective elbows!

What makes game special is the fact that it can, as Alexia Robinson of 'Game to Eat' says, 'be dressed up or down, served plainly or with low-fat sauces. Clever use of added ingredients means you could have an extensive range of great tasting dishes under the healthy option section'.

Eating game can improve your mood, make you less anxious and less tired – an extravagant claim to be sure, but it's all apparently down to the fact that certain game-bird meats, such as partridge and pheasant, contain selenium – a trace element now proven to influence the way the brain reacts. It is also thought to help protect against heart disease and cancer. A lack of iron can also leave you feeling tired and lacking in energy – one way of rectifying this particular deficiency is to eat venison, as its meat contains more than twice the amount of iron than is released from well-recognized iron-producing leafy green vegetables such as spinach – and it's a lot more interesting than taking a kelp tablet every day. The body needs a complexity of vitamins for a variety of reasons, many of which can be absorbed from fish such as trout and salmon. It's a disturbing fact that, even though there wasn't the selection of food in the shops fifty years ago, families were healthier then than they are now. Eating game seems a good way to begin making changes.

Then there is the moral aspect. Of course it is an undeniable fact that game birds are reared, salmon are farmed and some venison is commercially produced, but even so, the majority of game species has lived a life, however short, much as nature intended, free of the many stresses that cause concern regarding the care and welfare of many farm animals. For a great deal, if not all of that time, it has fed on an entirely natural diet containing no hormones or chemicals, which has got to be another good reason for choosing game products over meat produced on the majority of commercial farms (but certainly not all, as there are some excellent caring suppliers of organic produce).

So that's just a taste of why game is a good thing to put on the table, but can the average family (if there is such a thing!) afford to do so? In actual fact, the cost of game compares very favourably with other meats, and may, in some cases, actually be cheaper. In the 1980s, it was possible to sell shot pheasants and partridge, in the feather, for £5 per brace. Nowadays, most shoots will be lucky sell a brace for £1, and even taking into account the fact that there may be 'add-on' costs made by the game dealer and ultimate vendor, it is nowadays possible to buy an oven-ready bird for less than a fiver.

Availability is everything: a quick look in the farm shop shows that it is possible to pick up trout, salmon, pheasants, partridge, venison, guinea-fowl (which, although it is not shot is, to all intents and purposes, game) and, due to ever-increasing numbers, even wild boar. Look a little further – in the food halls of some of our larger agricultural shows, for example – and there is a good chance of coming away with a joint of something a little 'exotic', such as ostrich, kangaroo or crocodile, all of which possess the same 'healthy' qualities as the more usually seen game. Some types of game are a little more difficult to source. Woodcock and snipe are shot in such relatively small numbers that they are usually kept by those fortunate enough to bring one down – but who knows, one day you may be offered one and will be grateful for a recipe. If you want a wild goose and have neither the opportunity nor inclination to shoot one yourself, you will have to ask a wildfowler to get one for you, as, for some strange and probably archaic reason, they cannot be sold. As Mrs Beeton might have said, 'First catch your wildfowler'.

Game cooking is simple, but the particular leanness of some meats may produce problems in terms of dryness and toughness: there are, however, various ways of overcoming this, such as marinating; cooking hot and fast and serving 'pink'; resting the meat; and the obvious options of stews and casseroles.

Having somewhat sweepingly stated that game recipes of years ago mainly consisted of the bird or joint being roasted, go a little further back in history and it can be seen that chefs were more adventurous in providing variety and flavour: Louis XIV, 'The Sun King', for example, had a huge appetite for game dishes, often flavoured with herbs – possibly thus proving the old adage that 'there is nothing new under the sun'!

Cook Game takes the cook back to basics one minute and is mouth-wateringly adventurous the next. It perfects the already excellent and provides ideas, but above all, it aims to prove that game is adaptable, offering suggestions that range in origin from classic to contemporary and the Mediterranean to Milwaukee.

Pheasant

'That pheasant was pretty marvellous too,' Mr Candy said, by no means for the first time. He would never forget that pheasant: food of the gods, Manna, indeed.

(H. E. Bates, *A Little of What You Fancy*, 1970)

Undoubtedly the easiest game bird to obtain, oven-ready pheasants can be easily sourced from most butchers and quality supermarkets throughout the season. Farm shops will have fresh available between October through until the end of January and, thanks to new laws that came into being in August 2007, it should now be possible to buy frozen birds over a longer period than this. Game dealers will also supply to the public and usually have a shop attached to their commercial premises (find them in the Yellow Pages).

Increasingly, many private shoots are seeing the benefit of selling directly to the public, as, with the EU Hygiene laws that came into force on 1 January 2006, if you sell any game to an approved game-handling establishment (usually a game dealer approved by the Food Standards Agency), a nominated person involved in running a shoot must have attended a game-meat handling course and will, therefore, have proved that they possess 'sufficient knowledge of the pathology of wild game and of the production and handling of wild game meat after hunting'. Allied to this ruling is the need to possess a suitable 'game room' containing facilities for 'initial cooling, preparation of carcasses and temporary storage prior to sale or dispatch'. Having already had considerable financial outlay, it is but a short step for shoots to sell directly to the public, giving them the advantage of fresh birds and the provenance of knowing on which estate they have been shot.

Because of their cheapness and easy availability, don't be frightened to experiment with pheasant recipes: utilize the breasts in a special dinner or diced in a stir-fry, any way in fact, that you would use those of chicken or turkey. When only the breasts are required, skin rather than pluck – it saves a great deal of time. You can, if you wish, eviscerate the carcass, roughly 'chop' it and make stock.

Chilled Pheasant and Apple Soup

This is a good alternative to turning the carcasses left over from a meal of roast pheasant into game stock, and the combination of cider and apple purée gives the soup a 'sharp', rather than 'greasy' taste, which is so often evident in other cold game soups.

Serves 4–6
2 pheasant carcasses
2.25ltr/4pt water
570ml/1pt cider
1 onion and 1 carrot, both of which should be peeled
1 onion, peeled and chopped
1 large apple, peeled and chopped
1 tablespoon cider vinegar
30g/1oz butter
bouquet garni
seasoning
1 chicken stock cube
1 teaspoon cornflour
2 tablespoons crème fraîche

Place the pheasant carcasses, water, cider, onion, carrot, bouquet garni and stock cube into a pan and bring to the boil. Remove any residue that appears on the top of the liquid before reducing the heat and simmering for about two hours. Pour the contents through a fine sieve and into a clean pan. Boil and reduce the liquid until you are left with about 850ml/1½pt of your original quantity.

Meanwhile, melt the butter in another saucepan, add the chopped onion and apple, and sweat over a very low heat until they are soft. Add cider vinegar and liquidize well before bringing the contents to the stock. Mix the cornflour with water until you have created a paste and stir it into the soup until the latter begins to thicken. Put the soup to one side and allow it to cool before refrigerating until it is properly chilled. Just before serving, stir in the crème fraîche and garnish with watercress or basil.

Fruity 'Not-Quite-There' Pheasant Curry

This recipe is ideal for those who like the taste, texture and suggestion of a curry without the heat of a 'proper' one. The sweetness of the pineapple balances the taste of the curry powder.

Serves 4
4 pheasant breasts, skinned and sliced into 1cm/½in strips
1 tablespoon plain flour
1 mango
½ fresh pineapple
2.5cm/1in fresh ginger
3 shallots
2 tablespoons ghee or clarified butter (vegetable oil will do)
5 teaspoons curry powder
200ml/7fl oz stock
115ml/4fl oz natural yoghurt
2 tablespoons grated coconut
salt and pepper

In a polythene bag mix the flour, salt and pepper and pheasant strips until all of the meat is evenly coated. Peel the mango, pineapple, ginger and shallots. Cut the mango flesh from the stone, core the pineapple and cut both pieces of fruit into small cubes. Finely chop the ginger and the shallots.

Heat the ghee or oil in a large, heavy-bottomed frying pan and fry the pheasant pieces over a high heat until browned. Remove from the pan and set aside. Fry the shallots and ginger in the pan for 2 minutes. Add the fruit and curry powder and fry for 1 minute, stirring continually. Add the stock and bring to the boil before simmering for 5 minutes. Return the pheasant to the pan and stir in the yoghurt. Season, cover the pan and simmer for 5 minutes more. Meanwhile, dry-fry the grated coconut in a small frying pan over a high heat. Sprinkle over the curry before serving and garnish with mint.

Chestnut and Orange Pheasant Casserole

Chestnuts and pheasant seem to go together – maybe it's the association of autumnal woodlands in which both can be found. For convenience, this recipe uses frozen chestnuts, but imagine how much more pleasurable this recipe would be if the pheasants had come about as the result of a successful hour or two with the gun and the chestnuts picked fresh from the ground during the same foray.

Serves 4
4 pheasant breasts, cut into chunks
450g/1lb shallots, peeled
1 tin of game soup (or 425ml/¾pt game stock)
280ml/½pt red wine
280ml/½pt orange juice
450g/1lb frozen chestnuts
5 tablespoons thick-cut marmalade
salt and pepper
1 handful parsley, chopped

Place the pheasant chunks into a large casserole together with all the other ingredients *except* the chestnuts and parsley. Cover and cook in an oven pre-heated to gas mark 5, 190°C/375°F for 45 minutes. Add the chestnuts and continue cooking for a further 45–60 minutes or until tender and thoroughly cooked (actual timing will depend on whether frozen or fresh chestnuts are used). Sprinkle chopped parsley over the top and serve directly from the dish.

   NB To prepare fresh chestnuts, make a small slit in the skins with a sharp knife. Place in a pan, add sufficient water to cover and boil for 20 minutes. Drain the nuts into a colander and run cold water over them until they are cool enough to remove the skins.

Thai Green Pheasant

Serves 4
4 pheasant breasts, with the skin left on
1 jar Thai green curry paste
2 limes, halved
lime leaves
lemongrass stalks, halved lengthways
coriander

Rub the green curry paste all over the pheasant breasts, place them in a shallow container, cover with cling film and chill overnight.

Line a roasting tin with foil and place the breasts in, skin-side up. Roast at gas mark 8, 230°C/450°F for 30–40 minutes or until crisp. Arrange the lime leaves and lemongrass stalks on a serving dish and place the pheasant on top, and drizzle the cooking juices over. Add the halved limes; finish with a sprinkle of coriander and serve with noodles.

Spanish Pheasant and Chestnut Autumn Stew

This is another recipe, this time Spanish-based, that uses chestnuts.

Serves 4
2 small pheasants, jointed so that breasts and legs are separated
225g/8oz thick bacon rashers, cut into pieces
225g/8oz boiled chestnuts, roughly chopped
1 onion and 1 carrot, both finely chopped
1 × 400g/14oz tin drained plum tomatoes, roughly mashed
280ml/½pt dry white wine
4 bay leaves
4 cloves, roughly ground in a pestle and mortar
3 garlic cloves, sliced
2 sprigs fresh thyme
1 stick cinnamon
½ teaspoon paprika
olive oil

In a large saucepan or flameproof casserole, fry the bacon in 3 tablespoons of olive oil until it begins to colour. Add the onion, carrot, garlic, bay leaves and cinnamon, and cook for 5–10 minutes or until they begin to caramelize. Introduce the thyme, paprika and cloves, stirring constantly for a minute, before adding the tomatoes and cooking for a further 5 minutes, stirring occasionally.

In a frying pan, brown off all the pheasant joints in olive oil until they are sealed on all sides. Add the leg sections to the saucepan, pour in the white wine and simmer gently under a loose lid for about half an hour or until the meat feels tender when speared with the point of a sharp knife. Then add the chestnuts and the pheasant breast joints and continue cooking for a further 10–15 minutes. Check for seasoning and let the stew rest for a few minutes, once all the meat appears ready. Serve with basmati rice.

French Pheasant with Country Topping

Similar to a rustic French *cassoulet*, this particular dish continues the continental theme by the addition of *pain de campagne* bread slices, French grainy mustard and haricot beans.

Serves 4
4 pheasant breasts
4 spicy venison sausages
115g/4oz bacon rashers (or, in keeping with the French connection, a packet of *lardons*)
425ml/¾pt game stock
140ml/¼pt red wine
1 ~300g tin haricot beans
1 ~300g tin green lentils
1 medium onion, peeled and finely chopped
3 cloves garlic, peeled and crushed
3 stems celery, trimmed and chopped
3 tablespoons olive oil
2 tablespoons French grainy mustard
1 tablespoon tomato purée
3–4 slices *pain de campagne* bread

In a frying pan, sauté the bacon pieces until crisp before transferring them to a casserole dish. Add a tablespoon of olive oil to the frying pan and brown off the pheasant breasts on both sides. Transfer to casserole. Do the same to the sausages.

Add another tablespoon of oil to the frying pan and add the onion and celery, softening and gently browning both for about 10 minutes. Stir in the crushed garlic and, with a perforated spoon, transfer the vegetables to the casserole dish. Put both the wine and tomato purée into the frying pan and bring to the boil. Add, together with the stock, to the casserole dish, which should then be covered and placed in an oven at gas mark 4, 180°C/350°F for 30–40 minutes, or until the breasts are tender.

Drain and add the contents of both tins of lentils and beans before returning them to the oven until the casserole is once again bubbling. In the meantime, mix the mustard and the remaining tablespoon of oil and spread the resultant mixture on one side of each slice of *pain de campagne*. Place the slices mixture-side up on top of the *cassoulet* and continue cooking in the oven (with the casserole dish lid removed) for a further 10 minutes or until the topping is crunchy and brown.

Pan-Fried Pheasant Breasts in Bacon

Serves 4
4 pheasant breasts
4 slices of bacon
1 small tub soft herb and garlic cheese
55g/2oz butter (or a good 'glug' of olive oil)

Gently flatten each pheasant breast with the palm of your hand and make a pocket in each one with a sharp knife. Place a good teaspoon of herb and garlic cheese in the pocket created and wrap a rasher of bacon, spiral-fashion, around the breast, securing it, if necessary, with a wooden cocktail stick.

Put the butter or oil in a large heavy-bottomed frying pan and bring up to heat, taking care, if using butter, that it doesn't burn. Gently fry the pheasant breasts, turning frequently and occasionally inserting the point of the knife to check on cooking progress in the thickest part of the meat. Serve hot and with suitable accompaniments (*see* Chapter 14).

Fruity, Nutty Pheasant

Over the years, variations on this recipe (which we are led to believe actually began life in Russia) have been reproduced by many famous cooks. The reason that they are attracted towards it is probably the unusual mix of tea, grapes and walnuts. This is, therefore, our variation on a theme.

Serves 4
1 large pheasant
2 teaspoons China tea
450g/1lb white grapes
115g/4oz walnuts
140ml/¼pt white dessert wine
140ml/¼pt fresh orange juice
55g/2oz butter
salt and pepper

Make a cup of tea by pouring 115ml/4fl oz boiling water over the China tea and set to one side in order to infuse. Put half the butter inside the pheasant and place the bird into a fairly tight casserole dish. Crush the grapes through a wide-meshed sieve over the pheasant, before adding the strained tea, orange juice, white wine and walnuts. Season and cover with a tight-fitting lid so that the 'steam' cannot escape and place in an oven set to gas mark 4, 180°C/350°F. Some recipes suggest that this dish can also be done very successfully by simmering the casserole on a hotplate.

Whatever method is chosen, remove the pheasant from the dish after about 45 minutes and joint into four pieces. Put the bird to one side, whilst at the same time keeping it hot. On the hotplate, reduce the liquid until it creates a thick sauce, stirring or whisking constantly. Add the remaining butter at the very last minute and either pour the sauce over the pheasant pieces or serve in a separate jug. Serve with mashed potato and celeriac.

Orchard and Onion Pheasant

This is another recipe that uses a combination of tastes, which seem to marry well together. Again, a whole pheasant is used and cooked in a casserole at an oven temperature of gas mark 4, 180°C/350°F.

Jointed after cooking, one large pheasant will serve 4, but for smaller birds, why not give your guests half a bird each? The quantities given are for the latter option.

2 small pheasants
1 large cooking apple
1–2 pears
2 large onions, peeled and cut into rings
280ml/½pt cider
570ml/1pt game stock
115g/4oz butter
1 tablespoon Demerara sugar
seasoning

Make a rough stuffing of half the apple, pears and onion and place it inside the birds. On the top of the oven, melt the butter in the casserole (taking care not to burn it) before adding the pheasants (breast-side up). Place the dish and its contents into the oven and cook for around 15 minutes before turning the birds on their sides, adding 4 tablespoons of cider and returning to the oven for another 15 minutes' cooking time. Turn breast-side down for a further 15 minutes and then turn onto the remaining side for 15 minutes. Finally, cook breast-side up again for between 20 and 30 minutes, or until the birds are ready.

During the last half an hour of cooking, fry the remaining onion rings in a little butter, add the apple, pears and sugar, and cook until they caramelize. Make sure that you use a big enough pan, bearing in mind that there is a fair quantity of liquid yet to be added. Pour in the stock and remaining cider, heating and stirring until the liquid has reduced to approximately half its original volume.

Once the pheasants are done, remove them from the oven, spoon out the stuffing and joint into either quarters or halves. Add the stuffing and the pan mixture of stock, cider, onions, apples and pears to the juices left in the casserole and cook for a few minutes before liquidizing and serving from a sauce-boat.

Braised Pheasant in Calvados, Elderflower and Pineapple

It was once famously said 'if you can't stand the heat, get out of the kitchen'. Take care when setting light to the Calvados in this recipe.

Serves 4
2 pheasants, jointed
1 small ripe pineapple
4 shallots, finely chopped
1 large eating apple
1 tablespoon Demerara sugar
4 tablespoons Calvados
2 teaspoons concentrated elderflower cordial
Tabasco sauce
55g/2oz butter
seasoning

Rub the pheasant joints in elderflower cordial, season and roll in a little flour before browning them in butter in a heavy-bottomed frying pan. Add the chopped shallots and fry until soft. Warm the Calvados in a pan and slowly spoon over the meat pieces before lighting. Carefully shake the pan and its contents until no flames can be seen and then place the pheasant joints into a casserole dish.

Skin, quarter and de-core the pineapple. Chop it finely before adding it to the frying pan together with the apple, sugar, seasoning and a few drops of Tabasco. Heat up the contents of the frying pan until they become soft. Pour into the casserole and cover before placing the dish into a low oven gas mark ¼, 110°C/225°F for around 1½ hours.

Remove the pheasant pieces and place on a warmed serving dish before bringing the liquid up to boil on the top of the oven in order to reduce it. Serve with either garlic mash or saffron rice, garden peas and sliced fried apples.

SOME ROASTING TIPS

- Allow one pheasant for two people.
- To add flavour to a simple roast pheasant, place a garlic clove, half an orange or onion, and parsley into the body cavity.
- To keep moist, place half a raw potato inside each bird and spread a little oil or butter on the breasts.
- Cook in a loosely-formed foil package until about 10 minutes before the end of the accepted cooking time (normally, around an hour).

Roast Pheasant

Game birds can, if you are not careful, be a very dry meat. For this reason when roasting pheasant, it pays to cover the breasts of each bird with rashers of streaky bacon or to fill the body cavity with good-quality pork sausage-meat stuffing. Alternatively, roast with moist ingredients surrounded by plenty of liquid – if the liquid is alcohol-based, so much the better!

Serves 4
2 large pheasants
85g/3oz dried apricots
85g/3oz dates, de-stoned and finely chopped
115ml/4fl oz dry white wine
50ml/2fl oz Grand Marnier
50ml/2fl oz lime juice
2 tablespoons sugar
2 teaspoons dried thyme, together with a little fresh thyme as garnish

Soak the apricots in boiling water and allow them to stand and swell for 10 minutes before draining and cutting into quarters. Place the wine, liqueur, lime juice and sugar in a small pan and simmer gently for 5 minutes. Brush the pheasants with oil and roast breast-side down at gas mark 6, 200°C/400°F for 20 minutes. Pour out any obvious fat residue from the roasting pan before turning the birds onto their backs and adding the apricots, dates, dried thyme and liqueur mixture. Roast at the same temperature for a further 20 minutes – adding up to 115ml/4fl oz water, if the liquid looks like evaporating. After cooking, let the pheasants rest and cool slightly before attempting to cut each bird in half. Serve with the apricot and date sauce, garnished with fresh thyme.

Roast Pheasant with Madeira

Serves 4

Smear the breasts of 2 pheasants with butter and place them on a rack in an open roasting pan. Cook in an oven set at gas mark 5, 190°C/375°F for 15 minutes. Add 8 tablespoons Madeira and continue to roast for a further 30 minutes, basting the birds every 10 minutes with the juices from the pan. About 15 minutes before serving, place 4 or 8 rounds of bread in the pan to brown and absorb the juices. Lay the pheasants on a bed of watercress, add the slices of bread, which should by now have the appearance of croutons, and garnish with lemon slices.

Tea-Leaf Smoked Pheasant Breasts

Normally these pheasant breasts would be served hot, with new potatoes and green vegetables, but left to cool and cut into thin shreds, served over strips of crudités, they also make a very easy starter with a distinct taste.

Serves 4
4 pheasant breasts, skinned
2 lemon or limes, thickly sliced
225g/8oz rice
225g/8oz Demerara sugar
contents of 8 teabags

Entirely line a wok with a sheet of aluminium foil, leaving sufficient to fold over in order to eventually squeeze all sides together and form a seal. Put the rice and sugar into the wok and scatter over them the contents of the teabags. Heat until smoking and cover with a second sheet of foil, cut just large enough to cover the rice, sugar and tea leaves. On this sheet, lay the pheasant breasts and lime/lemon slices, before folding over the edges of the bottom, larger piece of foil so as to form a large loose parcel and smoke the breasts for 15–20 minutes until cooked.

NB It is possible to place the rice, sugar and tea directly into the wok – using just one piece of foil on which to lay the meat before covering the wok with a lid – the sugar does, however, burn the bottom of the pan, making it very difficult to clean.

(The same smoking method also works well with fish such as trout.)

Pheasant Pâté

Take a quantity of cooked pheasant meat free of all bones and weigh it. Take half the weight of the pheasant of cooked ham and finely mince both before mixing together. Season with salt and freshly ground black pepper. Melt 30g/1oz of butter for every 115g/4oz of mixture – add 1 dessertspoon brandy for every 30g/1oz butter and pour into the pheasant and ham, mixing well. Chill well for several hours before serving with toast and salad or as a starter.

Pheasant Enchiladas

Serves 4
4 pheasant breasts, skinned
8 soft flour tortillas
400g/14oz tin tomatoes
1 red onion
½ Spanish onion
2 spring onions
2 cloves garlic
280ml/½pt stock
85g/3oz feta cheese
½ lettuce
3 sprigs coriander
1 lime
2 teaspoons chilli powder
1 teaspoon dried marjoram
olive oil
salt and pepper

Cut the pheasant breasts into strips and stir fry for 5 minutes in 2 tablespoons olive oil. Using a slotted spoon, remove the pheasant strips from the pan and keep warm. Drain the tomatoes. Peel and finely chop the Spanish onion and garlic. Add a further tablespoon of oil to the pan used for the pheasant and fry the onion and garlic for 3 minutes. Add the tomatoes, chilli powder, marjoram and stock and bring to the boil. Continue boiling for 15 minutes or until the sauce has reduced by roughly a third. Season to taste.

Wrap the tortillas in foil and bake at gas mark 4, 180°C/350°C for 10 minutes. Meanwhile, shred the lettuce and spring onions. Dice the feta cheese, then peel and finely slice the red onion.

Brush one side of each tortilla with the sauce, scatter the lettuce and pheasant on top. Roll up the tortillas and arrange on a serving plate. Spoon over the remaining sauce and scatter the cheese and red onion strands over the tortillas. Garnish with coriander, and the lime cut into wedges.

Pheasant and Roast Pepper Pasta

Serves 4
4 pheasant breasts, halved
285g/10oz dried pappardelle pasta
2 red peppers, de-seeded and roughly sliced
2 green peppers, de-seeded and roughly sliced
4 tomatoes, halved

3 cloves garlic
5 tablespoons dry white wine
45g/1½oz butter
2 tablespoons olive oil
3 tablespoons chopped coriander
1½ teaspoons crushed cumin seeds
seasoning

In the bottom of a roasting tin toss together the peppers, garlic, a little of the olive oil, a tablespoon of wine and the crushed cumin seeds. Level off, season and roast in the oven at gas mark 6, 200°C/400°F for 20 minutes, stirring in the halved tomatoes halfway through.

At the same time, heat the remaining oil in a frying pan and fry the pheasant breasts for 1 minute each side over a high heat until browned. Add to the roasting tin, integrating them with the roasting peppers and garlic. Return to the oven for a further 10 minutes' cooking time. Remove the breasts, slice and keep warm.

Cook the pappardelle pasta in a large saucepan as per the manufacturer's instructions. Drain. Return to pan and toss with butter. Add the sliced pheasant pieces, chopped coriander and contents (including juices) of the roasting tin. Serve immediately.

Pheasant and Pancetta Rolls

This probably works best as a barbecue recipe and is a good way of using any pheasant breasts that may have been lurking in the freezer since the end of the game season.

Serves 4
4 large pheasant breasts, skinned
24 slices pancetta or prosciutto ham
1 clove garlic, crushed
1 tablespoon oregano leaves, chopped
85g/3oz softened butter
seasoning

Cut the pheasant breasts in half, lengthways. Place each piece between two sheets of cling film and gently flatten with a rolling pin or meat mallet. Mix the butter, garlic, oregano and seasoning together before spreading half the mixture over each fillet of pheasant. Lay 3 slices of pancetta on top of each piece. Gently fold each fillet into a roll, tucking in any loose bits as you do so. Tie with fine butcher's string to hold the rolls in place and, finally, smear the remainder of the 'stuffing' mixture around the outsides of each. Cook over medium-hot charcoal until tender (approximately 20 minutes) and slice each into 1.25cm/½in rounds to serve.

Pheasant and Endive Salad

For a stunning looking salad, simply arrange endive leaves into a star shape and lay thin strips of cold pheasant breasts at the tip of each leaf.

Partridge

The English partridge is, I think a delicious bird to eat and a joy and pleasure to everybody.

(The 6th Earl of Carnarvon, *Ermine Tales*, 1980)

For a variety of reasons, it is nowadays quite a simple matter to get hold of a brace or two of partridges for use in game cooking, but it has not always been the case. At first, there was only the grey or English partridge (*Perdix perdix*), which survived well with careful management on the majority of low-ground estates, especially those in the eastern counties. After the Second World War, however, as the countryside economy went into decline, so too did the fortunes of the wild grey partridge – relying as it does on an abundance of insect larvae with which to feed its young chicks; the introduction of herbicides also did not help.

Enter the red-leg or French partridge (*Alectoris rufa*): a bird introduced to this country due to its ability to breed well artificially and to be more easily managed on the sporting estate. In the mid-1960s, another type was brought into the UK, again from the continent. The chukar (*Alectoris chukar*) is, as can be seen from the Latin name, a close relative of the red-leg, was easily flock-mated by commercial game farms, laid even more eggs than the red-leg and could, therefore, be sold more cheaply to the ever-increasing numbers of shoots. The chukar was bred with the red-leg, but for various reasons well outside the scope of this book, the chukar was eventually superseded by the red-leg. It is, therefore, the red-leg that appears most regularly for sale and is most likely to be encountered by those wishing to *Cook Game*.

If, however, you ever have the opportunity to purchase grey partridge, do so: the purists think, along with the late Earl of Carnarvon, that it is far superior – it seems he was in good company as Winston Churchill is famously known to have liked half a cold roast English partridge for his breakfast, along with a glass or two of champagne!

Partridge and Pea Risotto Soup

Serves 4
250g/9oz cooked partridge breasts, skinned and shredded
340g/12oz frozen peas, defrosted
1.1ltr/2pt game, chicken or vegetable stock
170g/6oz risotto rice
1 onion, finely chopped
55g/2oz butter
4 tablespoons grated Parmesan
2 tablespoons flat-leaved parsley, chopped
freshly ground black pepper

Cook the onion in butter in a pan for 5 minutes until it starts to soften. In a food processor, purée half the peas. Add the risotto rice to the pan and stir to coat in butter. Pour in the stock and add all the peas and partridge meat. Simmer gently without a lid for about 20 minutes before seasoning to taste and scattering with parsley, grated Parmesan and freshly ground black pepper.

Sherried Cream Partridge Livers

Possessing such small livers, this recipe can only be attempted if you have a plentiful supply of partridge. It may be possible to save and freeze them throughout the shooting season until you have sufficient. You can, however, add those of pheasant or even a few chicken livers to make up the required weight. It makes an interesting and slightly different dish and the quantities given would serve 4 people as a starter.

Serves 4
225g/8oz livers
100ml/3½fl oz sherry
140ml/¼pt fresh soured cream
70ml/2fl oz stock
30g/1oz butter
55g/2oz seedless grapes (black or green, or substitute with half the weight of sultanas)
30g/1oz plain flour
seasoning

Dust the livers in seasoned flour and fry in melted butter for 3 minutes, tossing frequently. Gently stir in the sherry and stock and simmer for 2 minutes. Add the grapes, which should be halved, and the cream. Continue to heat gently and serve either on triangles of fried bread or over quenelles of rice.

Partridge Pot-Roast

The livers of partridge also feature in this recipe, which is slightly unusual in that the birds are pot-roasted in milk rather than stock. For a team of hearty eaters, give each person a bird each.

Heat 1 tablespoon olive oil in a flameproof casserole and brown 4 partridges. Add 2 large onions, cut into quarters, and 8 small tomatoes. Cook for 5 minutes before adding 280ml/½pt water, 280ml/½pt milk, 140ml/¼pt sherry, and seasoning. Simmer gently whilst pounding together the partridge livers and 2 tablespoons each of capers, parsley and pitted olives. Add to the casserole, cover tightly and cook in the oven at gas mark 2, 150°C/300°F for around 2 hours, or until the partridges feel tender when poked with the point of a sharp kitchen knife.

Simple Poached Partridge

As with the previous recipe, I am assuming one bird per person.

Place 4 whole partridges in a flameproof casserole dish or large saucepan. Peel and roughly chop an onion, a carrot, a stick of celery, a fennel bulb and add to the pot; together with half a dozen sprigs of fresh parsley, 280ml/½pt white wine and sufficient water to just cover the partridges. Poach gently for between 1–2 hours, depending on the age of the birds being used. Use the fennel bulb as garnish by cutting it into slivers. Serve as is, with a little of the poaching liquor or, alternatively, with one of the several suitable sauces to be found in Chapter 15.

Partridge, Pimms and Plums

Although this is a very quick dish to cook, to get the best out of all the ingredients, the partridge breasts need to marinate for several hours.

Serves 4
8 partridge breasts
225g/8oz plums, de-stoned and halved
1 clove garlic, peeled and crushed
4 tablespoons unsweetened apple juice
3 tablespoons Pimms
3 tablespoons soy sauce
1 tablespoon oil
¼ teaspoon dried thyme
15g/½oz butter
seasoning

Make a marinade of the apple juice, soy sauce, Pimms, garlic and thyme. Place the partridge breasts in a large shallow dish and cover with the marinade. Leave somewhere cool for several hours or, preferably, overnight.

Remove the breasts and reserve the marinade. Heat the oil and butter in a frying pan and fry the partridge pieces on both sides until browned. Add the plums, marinade and seasoning. Cover, stir occasionally and simmer gently for 10 minutes or until the breasts feel tender when poked with the point of a sharp knife.

Partridge and Kumquat Casserole

The addition of whole cloves of garlic makes this a dish that all diners should try if there's to be any kissing going on later! Add or subtract the numbers of garlic cloves, depending on your personal taste.

Serves 4
2 partridges
225g/8oz kumquats, each one halved
10 cloves garlic
2 bay leaves
425ml/¾pt dry cider
200ml/7fl oz apple juice
200ml/7fl oz double cream
30g/1oz butter
2 tablespoons olive oil
seasoning

Halve the partridges by cutting both sides of the backbone with secateurs or strong kitchen scissors and remove. Cut completely in half by cutting along one side of the breastbone. Cook the whole, unpeeled garlic cloves in salted boiling water for 4 minutes. Drain, cool and peel.

Heat the oil in an ovenproof casserole on the hotplate and then add the butter. When the butter begins to sizzle, add the partridge halves, skin-side down, and cook for 5 minutes or until golden brown. Remove to one side. Place the kumquats and garlic cloves in the same dish, tossing over the heat for a couple of minutes or until they too are golden brown. Return the partridge halves, add the bay leaves, cover and cook in the oven at gas mark 6, 200°C/400°F for 30 minutes. With a slotted spoon, lift the partridge pieces, kumquats and five of the garlic cloves onto a baking sheet. Cover with foil and keep warm.

Crush the remaining garlic cloves with the back of a wooden spoon. Add the cider and apple juice and boil for 5–10 minutes or until the sauce is syrupy. Remove from the heat and gently stir in the cream before bringing back to the boil and simmering for 1 minute. Return the partridge, kumquats and 5 garlic cloves to the sauce, cover and cook gently for a further 2 minutes.

Partridge, the Italian Way

This makes a good summertime lunch, especially when served with a crisp, dry Italian white wine such as Frascati.

For a more substantial winter evening meal, add chopped aubergines and sliced courgettes at the same time as you include the tomato halves. Serve them with mashed potatoes and seasonal vegetables.

Serves 4
2 partridges, halved
2 cloves garlic, peeled and roughly chopped
285g/10oz tomatoes
55g/2oz black olives, de-stoned
1 lemon
140ml/¼pt dry white wine
6 tablespoons olive oil
1 tablespoon tomato purée
1 tablespoon black peppercorns, crushed
1 sprig each of fresh rosemary and sage
pinch of salt

Make a marinade from the garlic, a few rosemary needles, pinch of salt, 3 tablespoons oil and the grated zest of the lemon. Rub it thoroughly into the breast side of the partridge halves before placing them in a shallow dish. Pour over the remainder of the marinade, cover with cling film and chill for at least an hour. Skin the tomatoes by plunging them in boiling water for a few minutes and then removing the peel. Cut in half and put to one side.

Heat the remaining oil in a large pan and fry the partridge pieces for around 10 minutes. Start breast-side down in order to seal the 'meaty' side first, but turn occasionally until all are nicely browned. Squeeze the juice from the lemon and mix with the tomato purée and wine, before pouring the resultant mixture over the meat. Stir in the tomato halves, cover and gently simmer for 20 minutes.

Remove the rosemary and sage leaves from their stalks and chop the leaves. Halve the olives and add to the partridge, together with the fresh herbs. Cover and simmer again for a further 5 minutes. Serve with warm crusty bread and a green salad.

Partridge Risotto

Serves 4
2 partridges
55g/2oz butter
1 peeled and chopped onion
115ml/4fl oz dry white wine
1.1ltr/2pt chicken or game stock
1 tablespoon olive oil
seasoning
285g/10oz Arborio rice
55g/2oz Parmesan cheese
handful of baby spinach leaves
handful rocket

Remove the breasts from the partridges and put them to one side. Skin the leg joints and slice the meat from the bone before chopping into small pieces. Melt the butter in a heavy-bottomed pan. Add the onion and partridge leg meat and cook gently for 5 minutes. Pour in the wine and boil rapidly until most of the liquid has evaporated. Then add the rice and cook, stirring until the juices coat all the grains. Add a ladle of heated stock and simmer, stirring until the rice has absorbed it. Continue slowly adding more stock until the rice is soft – probably after around 20 minutes.

Heat the olive oil in a frying pan and fry the partridge breasts for 3 minutes on each side until golden brown and no juices run out when pricked with a skewer or the point of a sharp knife. Remove to a chopping board and slice before stirring the cheese into the risotto. Once it has melted, add the spinach and rocket leaves and season to taste. Turn onto a serving dish and lay the sliced breast meat on top of the risotto. Garnish with a little fresh rocket and some grated cheese and serve immediately.

Partridge in Tarragon Sauce

A French neighbour gave me this recipe. He normally uses it with chicken, but I see no reason why it should not work equally as well, if not better, with partridge breasts. Tarragon has a strong and very individual flavour, so use it sparingly at first.

Serves 4
8–12 partridge breasts
85g/3oz butter
55g/2oz hard cheese (our French neighbour uses Cantal, but Cheddar is a good alternative)
30g/1oz flour
425ml/¾pt stock
140ml/5fl oz single cream
2 tablespoons tarragon vinegar
2 teaspoons French mustard
1 teaspoon fresh chopped tarragon or ½ teaspoon dried
seasoning

In a covered pan, gently cook the partridge breasts in 55g/2oz of the butter, for 10–15 minutes or until tender, turning occasionally. Meanwhile, melt the remaining butter in another pan, stir in the flour and create a roux before very gradually adding both the stock and the tarragon vinegar. Then stir in the mustard, tarragon and cheese; bring to the boil, still stirring continuously. Season and simmer for 3 minutes before removing from the heat and adding the cream. Heat gently without boiling. Place the partridge breasts on a serving dish and spoon over the sauce. Serve with new potatoes or rice and French beans.

Partridge Cutlets

Remove the breasts from 6 partridge and chop the meat into tiny cubes. Mix these with an equal amount of soft white breadcrumbs soaked in cream into which has been poured 1–2 tablespoons brandy. Season with a few grains of cayenne pepper and a little salt. Blend into the mixture 115g/4oz softened butter and the yolks of 4 eggs. Form into cutlet shapes about 7.5cm/3in long and 1.5cm/½in thick. Roll the cutlets in more breadcrumbs and sprinkle with just enough brandy to lightly moisten the crumbs. Fry in butter until the meat is cooked and the cutlets are golden brown. Serve with Raisin Sauce (*see* Chapter 15).

Partridge Breasts with Oyster Mushrooms and Chanterelles

Serves 4
8 partridge breasts
225g/8oz oyster mushrooms and chanterelles, mixed
1 clove garlic, finely chopped
1 tablespoon chives, very finely chopped
115ml/4fl oz dry white wine
2 tablespoons olive oil
55g/2oz butter
seasoning

Season the partridge breasts, heat the oil in a frying pan and cook the breasts, skin side down first, turning until each side is golden brown and the meat tender. Remove and keep warm. Heat the butter and fry the mixed mushrooms for 3–4 minutes. Add the garlic and the chives and cook for a further 2–3 minutes before adding the wine. Continue cooking until the wine has more or less disappeared. Lay the partridge breasts down the centre of a warmed oval serving dish, surround with mushrooms and take to the table immediately.

Partridges in their Nest

This is an adaptation of the classic French dish, *Perdix aux Chou*, less interestingly known in English as Partridge with Cabbage! Also known in some recipe books as Chartreuse of Partridge.

Serves 4
2 partridges (young, if you can get them)
225g/8oz streaky bacon, with the rind left on and roughly chopped
225g/8oz sausages, sliced
2 wide pieces of pork skin (which might be more difficult to get from an
English butcher's than it is from a French one)
1 Savoy cabbage, trimmed
2 small onions, each stuck with a clove
2–3 carrots, scraped and thickly sliced
425ml/¾pt game stock
115ml/4fl oz dry white wine
55g/2oz butter
1 teaspoon cornflour

Partridges in their nest.

Trim the cabbage and quarter, without cutting right through to the base. Blanch it in a large pan of boiling water for 10–15 minutes before running it under the cold tap and draining well. Stuff the partridges with the onions and, in a large casserole dish, brown them and the bacon in the butter. Remove both the partridges and the onions from the casserole and lay one of the strips of pork skin in the bottom. Place the cabbage on top (stalk-end down) and gently tease it open, making a 'nest' on which to lay the partridges and bacon. Arrange the carrots in with them and, if possible, bring back some of the cabbage leaves over the partridges, before placing the second piece of pork skin over the top. Add the seasoning, stock and wine. Cover tightly, wedging the lid with foil, if necessary, and cook at gas mark 2, 150°C/300°F for 2½–3 hours – checking that all is well after about an hour's cooking time has elapsed. About three-quarters of an hour before the end of the anticipated cooking time, quickly fry off the sausage slices in a small frying pan with a little oil and add them to the casserole dish. Remove the partridges when they are obviously cooked (it is probably easiest to carve them at this stage) and keep warm.

With two slotted spoons, lift the cabbage and its contents onto a large serving dish – let as much of the cooking liquid as possible drain off. Thicken the juices (which should still contain some pieces of bacon, sausage and carrot – although some will by now be integrated in the leaves of the cabbage) by adding the cornflour and finishing on the hob. Return the carved partridge meat to the centre of the cabbage 'nest', pour the sauce over and serve immediately.

Grouse, Snipe and Woodcock

…I suddenly came upon a grouse. The bird seemed bewildered… and flew, low and straight, into a five-barred gate. The bird was completely stunned… and I soon bagged it. Without the use of a gun, I had secured my grouse for dinner.

(Trevor Thornton-Berry writing in *The Field*, 1942;
reproduced in *The Changing Year*, 1993)

The Swedish playwright and novelist August Strindberg, apparently always ate his lunch at 3.00pm and the menu would often include 'ptarmigan and beer and fish dishes'. Ptarmigan, a close relative of the grouse is, however, unfortunately nowadays, very unlikely to find its way into the majority of kitchens. Grouse on the other hand are, and in some cases – it depends where in the country you live – are quite readily available from local game dealers and traditional family butchers. It is also becoming increasingly easy to buy oven-ready birds online during the season. In fact, due to the new Regulatory Reform (Game) Order that came into being on 1 August 2007, it should nowadays be possible to buy all manner of frozen game throughout the year. Young grouse will undoubtedly cost more, but are, depending on the particular recipe, often worth the extra expense.

Experienced guns can tell the age of a bird in several ways. If you obtain a grouse 'in the feather', for instance, look at the tips of its flight feathers: if they are rounded in shape, they are most likely to be old, but at first you may need examples of both young and old in order to compare. Another way is to hold the bird with its bottom beak between your finger and thumb – a young bird's beak will bend as a result of the weight of the body, whereas an old bird's beak will stay firm. Old birds may be shedding a toenail, but perhaps the most scientific method of aging grouse is to apply the Bursa Test (*see* Chapter 16).

Classic Roast Grouse

Allow one bird per person and put a knob of butter inside each bird, smear the outside generously with butter, cover with bacon and sprinkle with salt and pepper. Pour stock and red wine into a roasting dish, with the grouse on a trivet set above the liquid. Cook at gas mark 6, 200°C/400°F for 45 minutes, removing the bacon about 15 minutes from the end in order that the birds may brown. Use the juices for the gravy and serve with bread sauce. Garnish with watercress.

Casserole of Grouse

Old grouse can be cooked whole, with long slow braising. Vegetables and lentils make a useful addition to the pot in such a situation. Add red wine or port to the dish as you are cooking and/or use vegetable stock to provide moisture and a tenderizing effect. Redcurrant jelly is often used as an accompaniment to grouse, but in this instance it is incorporated into the final stages of the recipe.

Serves 4
2 grouse
1 onion, finely chopped
2 carrots, finely sliced
1 stick celery, finely sliced
115g/4oz button mushrooms
85g/3oz butter
280ml/½pt vegetable stock
115ml/4fl oz red wine or port
2 cloves garlic
1 bay leaf
4 sprigs thyme
1 tablespoon redcurrant jelly

In a flameproof casserole dish, brown the birds by frying in the butter. Remove and put the birds to one side. Fry the vegetables for a short while before adding the mushrooms, tossing frequently, for a couple of minutes and then add the red wine or port, stirring well. Add the herbs, garlic cloves and vegetable stock. Bring to the boil and return the grouse to the casserole dish. Cover and cook for an hour at gas mark 4, 180°C/350°F. Remove the birds and allow them to rest. As they cool, cut them lengthways down the backbone and keel (breast bone), to give each diner half a bird.

Meanwhile, strain the cooking juices into a saucepan, add the redcurrant jelly and reduce until the sauce thickens and takes on a shiny appearance. Pour over the grouse and serve with Turnip and Tarragon Rôsti (*see* Chapter 14).

Scottish Grouse and Haggis Stuffing

Make a stuffing by boiling a 450g/1lb haggis in a pan of water for half an hour. Drain and cut the 'skin' in order to remove the haggis filling, placing it in a mixing bowl. Mix in 170g/6oz fresh bread-crumbs, a beaten egg, seasoning and 2 tablespoons whisky.

Serves 4
2 grouse
1 onion, finely chopped
2 carrots, finely sliced
1 stick celery, finely sliced
1 small leek, finely chopped
85/3oz butter
280ml/½pt vegetable stock
280ml/½pt whisky
280ml/½pt whipping cream
2 cloves garlic, crushed
1 tablespoon juniper berries, crushed

Use the stuffing at the neck end, packing it well between the flesh and skin of the birds. Place any surplus inside the grouse. Season well and brown off the birds and fry the vegetables as for Casserole of Grouse. Return the birds to the dish; warm half the whisky in a small saucepan and, as it flames, pour over the grouse. When the flames have died out, add stock, garlic and the juniper berries. Cover and cook at gas mark 4, 180°C/350°F for around an hour, depending on the age of the birds. Remove the birds and allow them to rest. As they cool, cut them lengthways down the backbone and breastbone, giving each diner half a bird each.

Strain the cooking juices into a saucepan, boil to reduce and remove from the heat. Carefully add the remaining whisky and the cream, simmer and stir well. As with the Casserole of Grouse, pour the sauce over the birds and serve immediately.

Truffled Grouse

Assuming that you have a ready supply of grouse and you fancy treating yourself to an 85g/3oz black truffle, this is a mind-blowingly simple and delightful dish for 4 people.

Roast 2 grouse at gas mark 4, 180°C/350°F for 30 minutes (they should still be under-done at this stage). Cut off the breasts and thighs and leave to one side whilst you melt 55g/2oz butter in a large pan before adding seasoning together with 140ml/¼pt dry white wine. Place the grouse pieces in the pan and heat through for 2–3 minutes. Remove from the pan onto serving plates, pour over a little of the cooking juices, grate the truffle over the meat and serve immediately.

Grouse Soup

After removing the best bits of meat to make the Grouse Terrine or the Grouse Breast in Cream, place the carcass in a large pan and cover with water. Add 1 celery stalk and 6 sprigs of parsley, tied together, seasoning and 55g/2oz cooked chickpeas. Cover and bring to the boil before simmering for about an hour. Remove the bird from the pan and once it has cooled down, remove all available pieces of meat. Strain or sieve the stock into a bowl in order to ensure that you are left only with clear liquid.

In a frying pan, melt 55g/2oz butter and gently sweat 2 chopped onions and 2 diced carrots, simmering gently for 5–6 minutes and stirring frequently. Add the chopped pieces of grouse to the pan, together with 570m/1pt of the stock. Simmer for a further 10 minutes before blending in a liquidizer. Return to the pan and re-heat slowly, stirring all the time. The chickpeas should have ensured that the soup is reasonably thick, but if it is felt necessary to thicken at this stage, do so by adding a teaspoon of cornflour. Garnish with a swirl of cream, croutons, fresh chopped parsley or chives.

Grouse Breasts in Cream

Carolyn Little, writing in *The Game Cook* (Crowood, 1988 and 1998), offers this recipe saying that it is 'quite delicious', but makes the comment that it 'may seem unforgivably wasteful'. There are, however, ways in which the remainder of the birds can be used, such as in the Grouse Terrine and Grouse Soup.

Using 1 grouse per person, remove the breasts from each and place between a 'sandwich' of cling film on a wooden chopping board. Gently beat flat with either a rolling pin or meat mallet before cutting lengthways into 2.5cm/1in strips. Roll the breasts up tightly and coat them with flour, which has been seasoned with dried herbs, salt and pepper. Melt a little butter in a frying pan and gently cook the grouse for between 10–15 minutes or until it is golden brown. Pour fresh single cream over and heat well but very gently.

Carolyn suggests serving with plain boiled or sauté potatoes, asparagus, buttered broccoli and red cabbage.

Grouse, Grapes and Grappa

Serves 4
2 grouse
2 onions
2 carrots, chopped
2 sticks celery, chopped
285g/10oz sausage meat
2 stale bread rolls
115g/4oz butter
500g/1lb 2oz seedless red grapes
55ml/2fl oz Grappa (or French Eau de Vie)
olive oil

Soak the bread rolls in water. Slice one of the onions and sauté it in a saucepan with half of the butter. Introduce the sausage meat and fry until browned. Mix the ingredients of the pan together with the squeezed bread rolls, a few of the grapes and a little salt and pepper seasoning. Divide the mixture and use it to equally stuff the body cavities of both grouse.

Roughly chop the second onion and add to the carrots and celery. Brown the vegetables, together with the grouse, in a roasting tin with 4 tablespoons olive oil and the remainder of the butter; turn the birds to ensure that all sides are browned. Sprinkle the Grappa over the birds and roast at gas mark 6, 200°C/400°F for around 40–45 minutes. Add more grapes to the roasting tin before returning to the oven for a further 10 minutes. Transfer the grouse to a serving dish and allow them to rest before cutting into pieces. Serve together with the stuffing and a few fresh grapes as garnish, sprinkling the sieved cooking juices over the whole.

Grouse Terrine

A perfect starter and an ideal way of using up old grouse, should you ever have them. Roast birds slowly, following the basic principles as above, and when the carcass is cooled, pull off the best bits of meat from the breast and thighs. Boil the remainder to make stock. Freeze as a basis for grouse soup or other recipes requiring a game stock.

Serves 4–6
450g/1lb cooked grouse meat, roughly chopped
450g/1lb streaky bacon, remove any rind
450g/1lb black pudding, sliced or diced
225g/8oz minced pork
3 large onions, chopped
rind of an orange, thinly shredded
115ml/4fl oz brandy
30g/1oz butter
3 eggs, beaten

Place the grouse meat in a bowl, pour over brandy, cover with cling film and leave in a cool place overnight. Add to the grouse meat, the minced pork, the chopped onion, shredded orange, beaten eggs and then season. Fold together and mix well before then adding the black-pudding pieces. Line a 1.4ltr/2½pt terrine dish or straight-sided heatproof bowl with some of the bacon. Spoon in all of the combined meats and finish off the top by laying over more slices of bacon. Cover with greased foil or baking parchment. Stand the dish in a roasting tin or similar into which is poured hot, but not boiling, water until it reaches roughly halfway up the sides of the dish. Cook at gas mark 4, 180°C/350°F for approximately 1½ hours. Remove the covering and allow to chill completely before serving, either as slices accompanied by a green salad or with triangles of bread fried in butter.

SNIPE

Despite, or perhaps because of, its diminutive size, the snipe is a much sought after bird amongst sportsmen. To get anywhere near where they are feeding often involves some careful strategies and to actually be skilled enough to add one to the day's bag is quite an achievement – in fact, the term 'sniper' is thought to be derived from the fact that shooting the small jinking snipe is such a difficult feat, that it takes an excellent shot to do so.

In his book, *Border Reflections* (© HarperCollins, 1979), the former Prime Minister, Lord Home, remarked that, 'Anyhow there are sufficient to supply the connoisseur's delight which is a cold snipe with a poached egg for his breakfast.' Traditionally, woodcock and snipe are cooked plucked, but with their intestines remaining. The gizzard should, however, be removed (*see* Chapter 16). The customary way of cooking it is to grill the bird for about 10–15 minutes and then either serve it on toast or alongside an accompaniment of *pâté de foie gras*.

Some recipes require that the head is left on and the beak speared into the breast, but in this particular collection, the squeamish do not need to 'look away now'!

Woodcock.

Simple Snipe Bites

As a breakfast dish or more commonly as a starter.

Serves 4
8 snipe breasts
1 tablespoon olive oil
splash of lemon and a dash of brandy
salt and pepper

Heat the oil in a frying pan and sauté the breasts for 2–3 minutes each side. Season with salt and pepper, add the lemon and brandy and serve each breast immediately on a triangle of warm, buttered toast. For a starter, you might like to garnish with a little watercress and a lemon wedge, but for maximum flavour and appreciation, it is more important to get the Snipe Bites to your guests.

Roast Snipe or Woodcock

The following is the traditional way of roasting either snipe or woodcock. As always with either of these birds, allow 1 bird per person and, after plucking, do not draw the intestines from the birds as you would with any other form of game bird. Remove the gizzard as described in Helpful Hints (*see* Chapter 16) . To be a real traditionalist, the head should be plucked or skinned and left attached to the body. However, as I mention on page 229, there is no real benefit in doing so.

Place the bird(s), with the head tucked under, on a trivet in a roasting tin. Lay a rasher of bacon across the breasts and cook at gas mark 4, 180°C/350°F. (Woodcock will take approximately 25 minutes to get to the next stage: snipe only 15 minutes.) Remove the bacon rasher(s) and squeeze a little lemon juice over each bird before cooking for a further 10 minutes (both woodcock and snipe require the same amount of time for this stage).

Accompany with gravy made from the pan juices mixed with either a little game stock or white wine and serve with mashed potatoes, roast parsnips and green beans.

Snipe on a Skewer

In a variation of the above idea, this Italian recipe originally used freshly shot blackbirds and thrushes or whatever small birds were available. Provided that you can get the snipe, there is no reason not to use them as a substitute. I've never had sufficient to try this recipe as laid down here, but I've experimented with two woodcock and it worked very well.

Serves 4

8 snipe

10 slices of Italian or French-style crusty bread, sliced to about 1cm/½in thickness

10 slices pancetta, cut to the same shape as the bread slices

1 lemon

4 tablespoons olive oil

2 tablespoons Muscat wine

1 tablespoon finely chopped flat-leaved parsley

1 teaspoon honey

1 crushed clove of garlic

seasoning

Roast the snipe for around 10 minutes (15 minutes if using woodcock) at gas mark 9, 240°C/475°F. Remove from the oven and thread onto two long skewers, alternating them with the bread and pancetta.

Make a basting liquid by mixing together the juice of 1 lemon, 4 tablespoons olive oil, 2 tablespoons Muscat wine, 1 tablespoon finely chopped flat-leaved parsley, 1 teaspoon honey, 1 crushed clove of garlic and a little seasoning. Cook the skewered snipe over a barbecue or charcoal grill for 10 minutes, turning frequently and basting almost constantly with the prepared liquid. When done, serve with the bread slices. As this dish has its origins in Northern Italy, the birds would have traditionally been served with polenta, a type of mashed cornmeal, which, when served in this way is known as *polenta-e uccelli*.

WOODCOCK

Lord Byron claimed to have 'no palate', but nevertheless, was fond of 'woodcock, lobsters and brandy'! In Regency times, young 'bucks' would often drop in at their London club in order to finish off their evening with a late-night dish of devilled game. This consisted of all manner of bones such as the backbone of a pheasant or the legs of wild duck or grouse, which had been doused in all manner of sauces and were traditionally eaten with the fingers. Nowadays, the term 'devilled' is used far more loosely in cooking and can describe any situation where the bird has been split along the backbone in the way of 'spatchcocking' (*see* Glossary).

Regency woodcock.

Regency Woodcock

Serves 4
4 woodcock
8 bacon rashers, chopped (or a packet of bacon *lardons*)
55g/2oz fresh breadcrumbs
1 tablespoon of olive oil or butter
1 dessertspoon flour
150ml/¼pt stock
55ml/2oz single cream
2 tablespoons red wine vinegar and a dash of vermouth
salt and pepper
Dijon mustard
Worcester sauce

First spatchcock your woodcock. Fry the bacon in the oil or butter, add the breadcrumbs and sauté until crisp. Remove from the heat. Grill the woodcock by placing them breast-side down, brushing them with melted butter and cooking for 5 minutes under a medium heat. Turn the birds over and brush the breast-side with more butter plus mustard and Worcester sauce. Season with salt and pepper and grill for a further 5–10 minutes or until the juice runs pink when the breasts are pricked with the point of a sharp knife. Place on a serving dish and transfer to the warming oven.

Sprinkle a little flour into the grill pan and add the stock, vinegar and vermouth in order to deglaze. Add the cream. Once the sauce is prepared, pour it over the woodcock and finish by spreading the bacon and breadcrumbs mixture over the top.

Woodcock Breasts in Cognac

Use 1 bird per person. Clean and draw the birds, reserving the livers for later. Tie a fairly thick rasher of bacon around each bird and roast them at gas mark 7, 220°C/425°F for 12 minutes, or until the bacon is golden brown. Discard the pork fat, remove the breasts from the woodcock and set them to one side. Chop up the carcasses very finely, put them into a small pan and flame them with 2 tablespoons of warmed Cognac. Chop the raw livers and add them, with the flambéed carcasses, to the juices in the roasting pan in which the birds were cooked. Heat the mixture thoroughly without allowing it to boil and rub it through a fine sieve. Add 4 tablespoons of Cognac. Sauté slices of bread in butter, arrange the woodcock breasts on top and pour the sauce over the meat.

Woodcock Perigordine

Woodcock and truffles obviously go well together, especially in France where, in some regions, both can be found in abundance. This is, therefore, another French recipe as kindly offered by our neighbour Maurice. In a cost-cutting exercise, you could try cooking the birds at the earthenware-pot stage with truffle-flavoured oil rather than real truffle slices – the subtle truffle taste will, however, not be as pronounced.

Serves 4
4 woodcock
85g/3oz black truffle, sliced
2 cloves garlic, peeled and halved
¼ pint/150ml game stock or white wine
30g/1oz butter

Smear the breasts of the birds with butter before cooking in a shallow roasting tray for around 10 minutes at gas mark 7, 220°C/425°F. For the next stage, Maurice insists that only an earthenware cooking-pot will do, around the inside of which he liberally rubs the halves of garlic. Place the woodcock in the cooking pot, place the sliced truffle around them and add a little game stock or white wine. Place the pot in the oven at the same temperature as before and cook for 10–15 minutes or until the woodcock are tender.

As a variation to this recipe, stuff each bird with duck pâté, into which has been mixed a little truffle oil (or a few thin shavings of the real thing), before proceeding in the same way as described above; remember to add a few minutes to the final cooking time as, obviously, stuffed birds take longer to cook through. To make it a truly French experience, sprinkle the birds with half a glass of Cognac at the end of cooking.

Grouse, Snipe and Woodcock Melange

Of all the game birds, it is likely that, despite grouse being available from some butchers and game dealers, the three types covered in this chapter will nevertheless be the least likely to come by. Also, even the regular field sportsperson may end up at the close of the shooting season with just the odd grouse, snipe or woodcock in their freezer. A grouse will undoubtedly make a meal for two, but as for the rest, they often get thrown at the bottom of the freezer and ignored because one bird isn't big enough to do anything with. I've given this recipe the title I have, simply because it is appropriate for the game-bird types in this chapter. There is, however, no reason why, as in the case of a game pie, the meat element shouldn't be made up of whatever odd pieces of game one happens to have available.

Serves 4
450g/1lb cooked game, sliced
2 onions, cut into rings
1 tablespoon hot curry powder
425g/15oz tin tomatoes, drained and chopped
115g/4oz Cheddar cheese, grated
4 eggs, hard-boiled and sliced
425ml/¾pt white sauce (*see* Chapter 15)
225g/8oz rice, boiled
30g/1oz butter

In a frying pan, melt the butter and gently cook the onions until soft but not browned. Sprinkle with the curry powder and mix together well before removing from the heat.

In the bottom of a lightly greased, large, round, straight-sided ovenproof dish, use half the quantities given and begin layering tomatoes, game slices, onions, cheese and hard-boiled egg slices. Repeat the process with the remainder of the ingredients so far mentioned. Finally, pour the white sauce over the melange and top off with the boiled rice. Cover the dish and cook in a pre-heated oven at gas mark 4, 180°C/350°F for 30–40 minutes.

Serve by inverting the dish onto a plate – all things being equal, it should retain the shape of the dish in which it was cooked!

Wildfowl

Let a goose, or any strong or fat wildfowl, be roasted with the addition of a small onion, and a pared lemon, in the inside; as this will draw out the strong fat, and give the bird a milder taste.

(Col. Peter Hawker, *Instructions to Young Sportsmen*, 1814)

Wildfowl of any type should, depending upon what it has been feeding, be a plump bird. Unfortunately, although there is a lot of weight and body, surprisingly little is worth bothering with and, in the majority of cases, it is probably easiest to skin a bird and use only the breasts. They do, however, roast particularly well and are less fatty than domestic ducks.

WILD DUCK

Has there ever been a better-known recipe than *duck a l'orange* – that strange title that combines a bit of English and a bit of French? It appeared frequently in the menus of many 1970s restaurants and, like prawn cocktail and Black Forest gateaux, was the height of sophistication!

Roast Mallard

When roasting mallard, allow 1 bird for 2 people. Smear the breast of the ducks with a thin layer of marmalade and insert half an onion and about 55g/2oz butter inside each mallard. Roast at an oven temperature of gas mark 7, 220°C/450°F for about 45 minutes (this cooking time is for 2 ducks – increase it if cooking more). Make a gravy by scraping off the pan juices and adding a few segments of pith-less oranges.

Mallard Breasts with Blueberry, Orange and Mint Salsa

A few years ago, 'Foresight', the Countryside Alliance, and the National Game Dealer's Association, produced a small booklet called *Discover the Great Taste of Game*, in the hope of encouraging and promoting the consumption of game. This is adapted from one of their suggestions in that booklet.

Serves 4
8 mallard breasts
2 oranges

Trim and score the skin of the duck breasts and place in a shallow bowl. Grate and squeeze over the top, the rind from one orange and the juice of two. Leave to marinade in the fridge for several hours.
 For the salsa:

200g/7oz blueberries
2 spring onions; cut into thin diagonal slices
1 orange
2 tablespoons mint leaves, chopped
pinch cinnamon
Tabasco sauce

Remove the peel and pith from the orange and cut each segment into pieces, reserving the juices. Place the blueberries, cinnamon and juice into a saucepan and heat gently until the berries have slightly softened. Allow to cool. Stir in the chopped orange segments, sliced spring onions, chopped mint and a few drops of Tabasco.
 Cook the duck breasts by adding a little oil to a frying pan and browning the breasts, skin-side down, for about 5 minutes. Pour off any excess fat, turn and cook the other side for around 3 minutes or until done. Serve with the salsa, new potatoes and summer vegetables.

Rhubarb Duck and Ginger

Serves 4
2 mallard
225g/8oz chopped rhubarb
15g/½oz grated fresh ginger
¼ teaspoon dried ginger
55g/2oz sugar
1 tablespoon butter
1 tablespoon orange juice

Preheat the oven to gas mark 6, 200°C/400°F. Halve the ducks lengthways along the breast and backbone and place the resulting four pieces on a rack set above a roasting tin. Cook for 45 minutes or until done to your particular preference (test by spearing the fleshiest part with a skewer or the point of a sharp knife). About 20 minutes before cooking is expected to be complete, place the rhubarb, sugar, orange juice, fresh and dried ginger into a saucepan and simmer until the rhubarb starts to disintegrate. At this point, strain though a sieve and return the resultant sauce back into the pan. Add the butter and stir. As soon as the last remnants of solid butter have dissolved, pour the sauce over the four halves of mallard, which should, by now, have been transferred to a serving dish.

Teal with Roasted Salsify and Sweetcorn Purée

Serves 4
2 teal
2 leeks, finely chopped
1 carrot, scraped and chopped
1 stick celery, chopped
corn from 2 cobs of sweetcorn (remove from cob by rubbing a knife down the length)
225g/8oz salsify, peeled and blanched
225g/8oz spinach (fresh, for preference)
bouquet garni
2 tablespoons olive oil
55g/2oz butter
1.1ltr/2pt stock
200ml/7fl oz cream
seasoning

Put stock, carrot, leeks, celery, seasoning and bouquet garni into a large saucepan and bring to the boil. Place the teal into the pan and bring to the boil once more before simmering for 10 minutes. Remove pan from heat and allow the contents to cool before lifting the ducks from the liquid. Strain the stock, discarding the vegetables and bouquet garni. Tip 280ml/½pt stock into a small pan and retain the rest for future use (it can be frozen).

Bring the small pan of stock to the boil and then add the sweetcorn. Simmer for 5–10 minutes, add the cream and boil again in order to reduce and thicken the liquid. Once this has occurred, put the pan to one side and allow the mixture to cool slightly before puréeing in a blender.

Put the blanched salsify into a roasting tin and sprinkle with the 2 tablespoons of olive oil before roasting in a pre-heated oven gas mark 6, 200°C/400°F for 10 minutes. Remove from oven, place the teal on the salsify and smear with butter before returning to the oven for a further 10 minutes' cooking time. Check that the birds are cooked by ensuring that the juices run clear when you stick the point of a sharp knife into the breast. Allow them to rest. As they are doing so, wilt the spinach in a large frying pan with just the smallest amount of water and re-heat the sweetcorn purée. Remove the duck breasts from the carcass, place spinach at the centre of a serving dish, arrange the salsify around the side, place the duck breasts in the centre of the spinach and dribble over some of the cooking juices. Serve immediately – not forgetting to pass round the sweetcorn purée.

Spit-Roasted Wild Duck

Serves 4
2 mallard
2 small eating apples, peeled and cored
2 small onions, each stuck with 2 cloves
2 shallots
1 celery stalk
4 sprigs parsley
115g/4oz butter
1 tablespoon gin
2 tablespoons Cognac
2–3 tablespoons red wine
ground black pepper
30g/1oz flour (for the roux)

Wipe the ducks inside and out with a cloth dipped in gin. Stuff each of the birds with 2 sprigs of parsley, 1 apple, 1 onion, 1 shallot, ½ stick of celery and 55g/2oz of butter. Sew up the opening with butcher's string and a large meat needle. Rub the ducks with a little butter and sprinkle them with black pepper. Roast rapidly on a rotary spit for 15–20 minutes (the flesh should be rare and slightly bloody).

Remove the ducks from the spit, put them on a heatproof plate, pour the Cognac over them and ignite. Once the flame has died out, carve the birds into serving portions and rest. In a pan, combine the juices from the carving, the drip-pan juices and 2–3 tablespoons of red wine. Stir in a roux made from 30g/1oz butter blended with 30g/1oz flour and cook the resultant sauce for a few minutes. Pour over the carved duck slices and serve immediately with Game Chips, celeriac and crunchy stir-fried cabbage.

Pan-Fried Saba Duck with Horseradish Celeriac Rôstis

As with the Spit-Roasted Wild Duck above, this is another recipe that goes well accompanied by celeriac.

Serves 4

Marinade 8 duck breasts in 3 tablespoons of Saba (grape juice based) for at least an hour. Meanwhile, mix together 750g/1lb 10oz celeriac and 750g/1lb 10oz of potatoes, all peeled and grated. Add 1 egg, 3–4 teaspoons of hot horseradish sauce, seasoning and mix. Fry 4 peeled and finely sliced shallots, until golden. Drain the shallots and then pan-fry the duck breasts before transferring them to an oven to cook at gas mark 6, 200°C/400°F for 10–15 minutes, then leave to rest in a warm place. Shape the celeriac and horseradish rôstis into rounds and fry in a little oil and butter until brown – finishing in the oven for 10 minutes or until cooked through. Serve with sugar snap peas and garnish with the shallots.

Teal with Cider and Apples

Serves 4
4 teal
2 small onions, skinned and halved
2 medium onions, skinned and chopped
1 large cooking apple, peeled and quartered
680g/1½lb mixed cooking and eating apples, peeled, cored and sliced
570ml/1pt dry cider
140ml/¼pt double cream
115g/4oz butter
seasoning

Stuff each duck with half a small onion and a quarter of apple. Heat the butter in a heavy casserole and brown the teal well. Remove and set to one side before adding the medium-sized onions to the casserole dish and softening gently – this should take about 5 minutes. Add the mixture of apple types, the cider and a little seasoning. Return the teal to the casserole dish, ensuring that they are all as much into the liquid mixture as possible. Cover and simmer very gently for around 1 hour or until the meat is tender. Remove the ducks and carve off the breasts before placing them on a serving dish (depending on your guests, you could serve the teal whole, directly onto a dinner plate), add the double cream to the sauce and spoon the mixture over and around the breast slices or whole duck. Serve with Parsnip Mash (*see* Chapter 14) and stir-fried cabbage.

Pot-Roasted Widgeon

The name widgeon is often spelt without the 'd'; one spelling is much older than the other, but it matters little which one is used, as both are correct. In the shooting world, it is usual to refer to widgeon, teal and the like in the singular, rather than saying 'widgeons', for example, in the plural.

Serves 4
2 widgeon
115g/4oz butter
2 shallots, chopped
1 clove garlic, crushed
1 bouquet garni
8 small dessert apples, peeled and cored
1 wine glass port
½ wine glass orange juice
3–4 tablespoons redcurrant jelly
2 tablespoons wine vinegar
seasoning

Melt half the butter in a flameproof casserole and brown the teal. Add the shallots, garlic and bouquet garni, cover and cook in the oven at gas mark 4, 180°C/350°F for 40–50 minutes, basting occasionally. Bake the apples in the oven with the remainder of the butter until browned. Melt the jelly in the wine vinegar and coat the apples.

Once the widgeon are tender, cut them in half lengthways and keep warm. Skim any fat from the casserole, add the port and orange juice, season to taste and bring to the boil in order to reduce and thicken the sauce. Arrange the halved widgeon on a plate; pour over some of the sauce (serving the remainder in a sauce boat or gravy jug). Serve the baked apples separately.

Duck Breast Salad with Raspberry Dressing

Any type of duck breast can be used in this colourful and extremely tasty recipe, which was given to me by the wife of an enthusiastic sporting doctor.

You could make your own raspberry vinegar by filling a Kilner jar with fruit, topping up with white wine vinegar and leaving in a sunny, warm position for a couple of weeks. Strain out the fruit so that you are left with pure liquid. Bottle and store.

Duck breast salad with raspberry dressing.

Serves 4
2 mallard or 4 teal
115g/4oz raspberries (fresh or frozen)
55g/2oz crushed walnuts
2 avocados
1 tablespoon whole-grain mustard
1 tablespoon raspberry vinegar
1 tablespoon sugar
280ml/½pt olive oil
seasoning

Coat the ducks in a little oil and roast in an oven at a temperature of gas mark 7, 220°C/425°F for 25 minutes. Once cooked, remove the breasts and arrange on individual dinner plates. Spread a 'fan' of half a sliced avocado by each breast and sprinkle with raspberries and walnuts.

Make a dressing by mixing together the mustard, sugar, seasoning and raspberry vinegar before finally whisking in the olive oil. Dribble a little of the dressing over the duck meat. Accompany with a green salad (serve the remainder of the dressing in a jug so that it can be used on the salad) and supply plenty of fresh, preferably warm, French bread.

Duck Timbales

This makes a good starter, using up any pieces of pre-cooked duck meat left over from another meal.

Serves 6
115g/4oz cooked duck meat, finely chopped
115g/4oz fresh breadcrumbs
170ml/6fl oz milk
2 tablespoons sherry
whites of 3 eggs
1 teaspoon finely chopped shallots
1 teaspoon finely chopped parsley
seasoning made up of a pinch each, salt, pepper, and nutmeg

Place the breadcrumbs and milk in a pan and cook over a low heat for 4–5 minutes, or until the mixture looks like oatmeal. Remove from the heat; add the chopped shallots and parsley.

In a bowl, pour the sherry over the duck meat and leave to infuse before seasoning. Add the breadcrumb mixture and mix well before folding in the stiffly beaten whites of the eggs. Spoon into six individual buttered ramekin dishes or similar moulds, filling each two-thirds full. Put the dishes in a roasting tray of hot, but not boiling, water and bake in a moderate oven for 30 minutes. Remove and let the dishes stand for a few minutes before turning out onto individual starter plates. For colour, try setting them on a base of creamed spinach. Serve with triangles of bread fried in butter.

WILD GOOSE
Goose as a meat is at its best in the first year. It is moist and tasty with its own individual and unique taste. Once geese begin to mate or lay, however, the quality of the flesh toughens and will never really regain its delicacy. It is possible to use goose breasts for virtually any recipe normally associated with beef.

Stuffed Goose Breast

Use 1 goose breast per person. The somewhat casual quantities given here are for 2 people.

Slit open goose breasts with the point of a sharp knife in order to form a 'pocket' in each. Make a stuffing mix from sausage meat, a peeled, cored and finely chopped cooking apple, plus a finely chopped red onion and a finely chopped handful of dried apricots. Add a little seasoning of salt and pepper.

Fill the pockets in the breasts with stuffing, packing in as much as possible. Using butcher's string and a large meat needle, sew together the edges of the goose breast to keep the stuffing firmly in place. Wrap loosely in tin foil so that, during cooking, steam will be able to circulate around the meat. Bake in an oven at gas mark ½, 120°C/250°F for approximately 1 hour. Unwrap and baste occasionally. Serve hot or cold.

Crispy Goose Tex-Mex Casserole

Were it not for the cooking time, this simple and unusual recipe could equally have appeared in Fast Food – Feed the Kids (*see* Chapter 11).

Serves 4
450g/1lb minced goose breast
410g/14oz tin tomatoes
425g/14oz tin red kidney beans
500g/1lb 2oz potatoes, thinly sliced
115g/4oz grated Cheddar cheese
50g pack corn chips
1 tablespoon olive oil
¼ teaspoon cumin powder

Heat the oil in a heavy-bottomed frying pan and fry the minced goose breast for 5 minutes before adding the tomatoes, drained beans and cumin powder. Turn down the heat and simmer for 15 minutes, stirring occasionally. In a bowl, mix the sliced potatoes and half of the cup of grated cheese. Layer approximately a third of the potatoes/cheese on the base of an ovenproof dish and add half of the mince mixture. Top with another potato layer, another one of mince and finish off with potatoes. Bake at gas mark 4, 180°C/350°F for 45 minutes. Remove and spread the remainder of the cheese plus the contents of the corn chips packet over the top before baking at the same temperature for another 15 minutes.

Roast Goose

To roast a wild goose, dry the skin thoroughly with kitchen paper, both inside and out, and prick all over with a fork to help release the fat during cooking. Pre-heat the oven to gas mark 8, 230°C/450°F. Rub the goose with a tablespoon of fine sea salt and lay on a rack in a roasting tray, breast-side down. Stuff the cavity of the bird with whole onions and/or apples, if you like, but remember that any kind of stuffing may well prolong the cooking times necessary. Roast at a high temperature for 20 minutes, then turn the bird over and roast for a similar amount of time or until the skin is a light mahogany colour and beginning to crisp. Turn the oven down to gas mark 4, 180°C/350°F and cook for a further 1½–2 hours. When the goose is cooked, leave to rest for a while, loosely covered by aluminium foil.

Wild Goose Stew

Serves 4
1 goose
115g/4oz streaky bacon, roughly chopped
2 onions, peeled and sliced
225g/8oz mushrooms, roughly chopped
3 sprigs parsley
1 bay leaf
1 clove garlic
140ml/¼pt brandy
425ml/¾pt claret
pinch thyme
seasoning

Cut the goose breasts into chunks and place them into a bowl or deep-sided dish. Add seasoning, bay leaf, onions, parsley and thyme, together with the brandy and claret. Let the meat marinade for several hours, but, ideally, overnight.

Put the bacon into a casserole dish and heat for 10 minutes in a hot oven (gas mark 7, 220°C/425°F). Remove the goose pieces from the marinade and add to the casserole. Bake for 15 minutes, turning the pieces frequently so as to brown all sides, then add the marinade, the garlic clove (crushed) and the chopped mushrooms. Pour on sufficient boiling water to cover the meat well. Place the lid on the casserole, reduce the oven temperature to gas mark 3, 160°C/325°F and simmer the stew for around 1 hour or until the goose feels tender. Add more water to the casserole during cooking, if felt necessary. Serve directly from the cooking dish onto plates of wild rice.

Goose Provençale

Most game is dry and lean of flesh – although the wild goose is not as 'fatty' as its farmyard cousin, this particular roast will be enhanced if the bird is cooked on a rack over a roasting tin and basted frequently, rather than leaving it to cook in its own fat.

Serves 4
1 goose
12 ripe olives soaked in garlic-infused olive oil
1 onion, peeled and chopped
3 sticks celery
115g/4oz butter
140ml/¼pt red wine
170g/6oz toasted breadcrumbs
2 teaspoons Cognac
70ml/2½fl oz water
½ tablespoon cornflour
seasoning

In a skillet, sauté the onion and chopped celery in butter. Remove from the heat and add the bread-crumbs, olives, Cognac and seasoning. Mix together well and stuff the goose with the resulting mixture. Butter the breasts and sprinkle with a little sea salt and ground black pepper. Place the goose on a rack in a roasting tin and gently pour the wine and water over it – taking care not to dislodge all the seasoning from the buttered breasts. Roast in a very hot oven, gas mark 8, 230°C/450°F for about 45 minutes, depending upon the actual size of the goose. Baste the bird frequently with the pan juices and, when cooked, remove the bird to a warming oven or similar. Skim off most of the fat from the cooking juices and stir in the cornflour mixed to a paste with a drop or two of water. Stir until the gravy is smooth and slightly thickened. Serve separately in a gravy or sauceboat.

Young Wild Goose with Potato Stuffing

Mash 10 boiled potatoes, reserving the water in which they were cooked. Sauté 1 cup of chopped onions and a ½ cup of chopped celery in oil until they are partially cooked, but not brown. Stir the onions and celery into the potatoes, together with 4 slices of bread, crumbled, 2 beaten eggs and poultry seasoning. Stuff the goose and truss it. Roast the goose as above, basting it occasionally with the reserved potato water.

Wood Pigeon

Pigeons provide the highest number of days shooting in the UK and over
3½ million are shot annually in order to protect crops. Ninety per cent are
used for culinary purposes.
    (Figures obtained as a result of recent research carried out by PACEC.)

The research by Public & Corporate Economic Consultants (PACEC) suggests that wood pigeons are an easily accessible commodity and that they are obviously already well-used by many enthusiastic game-cookery aficionados. In certain parts of the country, wood pigeons can be a pest to the arable farmer and, depending on the time of year, can feed quite heavily on crops just coming 'into ear', or strip fields of greenstuffs when there is little natural food around.

Pigeon are not classified as game and are, therefore, available all the year round – there are some pigeon shooters who wish to have a 'close season' implemented but, for the moment, it should be relatively easy to find a local source of pigeon for use in the kitchen. If all else fails, you could try catching your own in the local park – it is said that when the novelist Ernest Hemingway was too poor to feed his family whilst living in Paris, he killed feral pigeons in the Luxembourg Gardens and took them home to eat, concealed in his son's pram!

Because of their size, most recipes suggest using just the breasts – this negates the need for plucking as, by removing just enough feathers to see the skin along the breastbone, it should be possible to insert the point of a sharp knife and remove the breasts leaving the skin attached to the feathers. Use the rest of the carcass to make a game stock.

A Marinade for Pigeons

No matter what the eventual recipe, pigeon breasts benefit from being marinated overnight. For four breasts, make a marinade out of 4 juniper berries, red wine to cover, sea salt and black ground pepper, one finely chopped onion and garlic. Or, use 2 chopped red onions, a mixture of herbs and equal quantities of red wine and vinegar sufficient to cover.

Grilled Pigeon

Young tender pigeons can be grilled if kept well basted. Place a small knob of butter inside the carcass and brush the breasts with melted butter before cooking under a moderately hot grill – not forgetting to occasionally coat with more butter. For the final 5 minutes of cooking time, add sections of grapefruit and garnish with cherries and lettuce before taking to the table.

To grill just the breasts, smear with butter and seasoning and cook under a hot heat for 5–10 minutes. For grilling either whole birds or breasts, experiment by marinating in a mixture of port, red wine, raisins, oil, fresh orange juice and zest.

Braised Pigeon with Orange

It is surprising just how many game recipes are associated with oranges. Duck is a classical and obvious one, but the citrus effect also works well with pigeons.

Serves 4
4 pigeons
4 small oranges
4 rashers bacon
4 shallots, chopped
55g/2oz butter
140ml/¼pt port or red wine
280ml/½pt stock
1 bouquet garni
½ teaspoon crushed coriander
1 tablespoon flour
2 tablespoons Cointreau
salt and pepper

With a potato peeler, remove some thin slices of zest from half the oranges and put to one side. Place an orange in the cavity of each bird and wrap a rasher of bacon around each pigeon, securing it in place by 'pinning' it with a wooden cocktail stick. Heat the butter in a large casserole and fry each bird until it is golden brown. Put them to one side and, in the same pan, fry the shallots. When they are also golden brown, stir in the flour and cook for 3 minutes before gradually stirring in the wine, stock and seasoning. Return the pigeons to the casserole and add the bouquet garni and the coriander. Cover and cook in the oven at gas mark 3, 170°C/325°F for 1½–2 hours or until the pigeons are tender.

As the pigeons are cooking, cut the orange zest into strips, place in a small pan with a little water and simmer gently for 15–20 minutes. Strain and reserve the strips.

Once the pigeons are cooked, transfer them to a serving dish. Strain the sauce and juices from the casserole into a saucepan – if necessary, thicken the sauce with the smallest amount of cornflour, remembering to stir constantly as you do so, otherwise you may end up with lumps. Assuming all is well, add the Cointreau to the sauce before pouring all over the pigeons. Sprinkle the orange strips over the birds and serve immediately.

Braised pigeon with orange.

Pigeon Pâté

To make a simple pigeon pâté, take 4 marinated, chopped pigeon breasts, 285g/10oz of sausage meat, 115g/4oz of chopped bacon and a few chopped herbs. Combine all the ingredients. Line a dish with 2 rashers of bacon and put the pâté mixture in the middle. Top with two more rashers. Cover with buttered greaseproof paper or kitchen foil and cook in a moderate oven for around 1½ hours or until the mixture has set. Serve cold with triangles of warm toast.

Quick and Easy Pigeon Cannelloni

The use of pre-packaged ingredients may cause this particular recipe to be frowned on by the cooking police, but it's a quick and tasty way of using up pigeon breasts that may otherwise linger in the freezer.

Serves 4
250g/9oz minced pigeon breast
1 small onion, finely chopped
250g/9oz packet frozen chopped spinach
1 small onion, finely chopped
130g tin sweetcorn, drained
130g tin diced capsicum, drained
250ml jar spaghetti sauce
120g packet dried cannelloni shells
140g jar cream cheese spread
2 tablespoons dried breadcrumbs
1 beaten egg
30g/1oz butter

Gently cook the spinach and onion in butter in a small frying pan for 10 minutes. Pour into a bowl and allow to cool. Using the same pan, add a little olive oil and cook the minced pigeon breasts for 3 minutes. Into the cooled spinach mix add the mince, sweetcorn, capsicum, breadcrumbs and egg. Spread some of the spaghetti sauce over the base of a shallow casserole dish. Spoon the filling mixture into the cannelloni shells and arrange them on top of the spaghetti sauce. Pour the remaining sauce over and dot with teaspoonfulls of cheese spread. Bake at gas mark 4, 180°C/350°F for 40 minutes. Leave to stand in a warm place for 5 minutes before serving.

Pigeon in Minutes

This recipe is so quick and simple, it could easily have found its way into Chapter 11, Fast Food – Feed the Kids. For the marinade, use either of the marinades described on page 68.

Serves 4
4 pigeon breasts cut into long thin strips and marinated
2 red onions, sliced
115g/4oz mushrooms
55g/2oz butter
140ml/¼pt crème fraîche

Soften the onions in butter, add the pigeon breasts and cook gently. Add the mushrooms and half the marinade. Cook gently again before finally adding the crème fraîche. Stir and serve with either Basmati or your own particular favourite type of rice. (When cooking rice, add a little oil to the water and fluff up with a fork immediately before serving.)

Pigeon Breasts in a Wild Mushroom Sauce

The highly successful 'Game's On' campaign (www.gameson.org.uk), which is encouraging more and more people to try game for the first time, produces some wonderful recipes, from which this is derived.

Serves 4
4 pigeons
225g/8oz wild mushrooms
½ onion, chopped
1 carrot, chopped
1 stick celery, chopped
bay leaf and thyme
1 tablespoon tomato purée
570ml/1pt chicken stock
1 miniature bottle brandy
olive oil
seasoning

Remove the breasts from the pigeon and put to one side. Roughly chop the remains of the carcass and legs. Fry quickly in a hot frying pan together with all the chopped vegetables until brown. Add the tomato purée and cook for a further 2 minutes. Add the brandy and flame. Add the chicken stock and herbs, simmer and reduce the volume by two-thirds. Strain and season before putting aside to keep warm.

Sauté the pigeon breasts in a little oil – both sides should be well done, whilst the centre remains slightly 'pink' – and leave to rest on a warm serving dish. Add a little more oil to the same pan and quickly fry the washed and seasoned mushrooms until brown. Cover the breasts with sauce and wild mushrooms and serve immediately.

Pigeon with Warmed Mushroom Salad

For this recipe, you do need whole pigeons, plucked and dressed.

Serves 4
2 pigeons
butter
115g/4oz cheese, finely grated
140ml/¼pt stock
seasoning
1 teaspoon mustard
1 teaspoon Worcester sauce
1 teaspoon mushroom ketchup
1 tablespoon brown sugar
2 tablespoons port

Season the pigeons well and smear with butter. Lay them in a roasting tin and place in the oven at gas mark 7, 220°C/425°F for 20 minutes. Afterwards, cut each pigeon in half lengthways and place in a casserole. Sprinkle with cheese and moisten with stock before covering and cooking at gas mark 3, 160°C/325°F for 45 minutes. Meanwhile, mix together the mustard, Worcester sauce, brown sugar, mushroom ketchup and port.

When the pigeon halves are cooked, transfer them to a serving plate. Pour the mixed sauce ingredients into the casserole and bring to the boil before pouring over the birds.

For the Warmed Mushroom Salad:

2 tablespoons olive oil or, to make this recipe even more interesting, any subtle nut-flavoured oil
1 medium onion, finely chopped
1 garlic clove, peeled and chopped
2 red chillies, de-seeded and sliced
1 large flat or field mushroom, wiped and sliced
55g/2oz each of oyster mushrooms, shitake, enoki and one other of your choice
2 teaspoons toasted sesame seeds
a few leaves of flat-leaf parsley

Heat oil in a pan and fry the onion, garlic and chillies until they are soft but not discoloured. Add the sliced flat mushroom, season and mix together gently before adding the selection of exotic mushrooms and cooking until tender. Serve with the pigeon, having first sprinkled the mushrooms with toasted sesame seeds and garnished with the parsley leaves.

Pigeon with Tomato and Chocolate Sauce

Serves 4
4 pigeons
4 rashers bacon, chopped
2 large onions, sliced
2 carrots, diced
2 beef tomatoes, skinned and chopped
2 cloves garlic, crushed
beef or game stock
1 glass dry sherry
1 tablespoon sherry (or wine) vinegar
375g/12oz packet dried noodles
1 tablespoon chopped parsley
2 cloves
nutmeg, grated
2–3 teaspoons grated bitter chocolate

Brown the pigeons and bacon in a little oil, before placing them breast-down, in a flame-resistant casserole dish. Spoon in the onions and add the carrots, garlic, cloves, parsley, seasoning and a little grated nutmeg. Add the vinegar and just enough stock to cover. Bring to the boil, cover the casserole dish and simmer until the pigeon breasts feel tender when poked with the point of a sharp knife. Remove the breasts and keep warm. Blend the sauce in a liquidizer and bring back to the heat, very slowly adding both the sherry and the grated chocolate. Simmer for a further 10 minutes, stirring frequently. On individual serving plates lay a bed of buttered noodles and place two pigeon breasts on each. Finish off by pouring the sauce over the breasts.

Petit Pigeon Puddings

This makes a good starter, or try serving two puddings to each person together with buttered new potatoes and salad as a lunchtime meal. The quantities given should make about 8 puddings.

2 pigeons
2 rashers bacon
2 shallots, peeled, but left whole
10 crushed juniper berries (use a pestle and mortar or the end of a wooden rolling pin)
4 teaspoons redcurrant jelly
570ml/1pt water
2 teaspoons aspic granules
55g/2oz butter
1 tablespoon crème fraîche
½ teaspoon very finely crushed dried bay leaf
30g/1oz softened butter
seasoning

Cook the pigeons by smearing their breasts with the butter and laying a rasher of bacon over the top. Stuff each bird with a shallot, a spoon of redcurrant jelly and a quarter the quantity of crushed juniper berries. Season and loosely wrap together in tin foil to make a parcel before placing in a shallow roasting tin and cooking for 1½ hours at gas mark 3, 160°C/325°F. Allow to cool and remove the breasts and as much of the flesh as is practicable. Roughly chop and put to one side.

Place the pigeon carcasses in a pan, together with the water and simmer until the liquid has reduced by half. Remove the pigeons and discard. Strain the juice and bring back to the boil before adding the aspic granules and stirring until they are completely dissolved.

Place the pigeon meat, the liquid, the remaining juniper berries and redcurrant jelly, the crème fraîche and crushed bay leaf (leaves) into a food processor and blend until the mixture is smooth and creamy. Lightly grease 8 ramekin or similar small dishes, spoon in the mixture and leave to cool before chilling in the fridge. When completely set, turn out onto individual plates and serve garnished with a little flat-leafed parsley or watercress.

Pigeon 'Scampi'

Serves 4
450g/1lb pigeon breasts, cut into long thin strips
55g/2oz butter
115g/4oz mushrooms, wiped and sliced
3 tomatoes, skinned and sliced
3 shallots, peeled and sliced
1 garlic clove, peeled and crushed
bouquet garni
1 glass dry white wine
280ml/½pt stock
1 teaspoon concentrated tomato purée
flour

Simmer the shallots and the bouquet garni with the wine until the mixture has reduced by half. Remove the bouquet garni. In another pan, melt half the butter, add 30g/1oz flour and stir into a roux before adding garlic, tomato purée and stock. Simmer for 5–10 minutes. Pour in wine mixture and cook for a further 5 minutes.

Meanwhile, roll the pigeon pieces in flour and sauté in the remaining butter for 5 minutes, tossing frequently. Sauté the mushrooms and add to the sauce, together with the tomatoes. Re-heat the sauce for a minute or two and spoon over the pigeon 'scampi'. Serve over a bed of rice or noodles.

Pigeon Almondine

This is apparently, an American recipe, given to us by a much-travelled 'backwoods-man'. In its home country, it is more usual to use quail or doves, but we are assured that this has been 'tried and tested' with wood pigeon and 'very nice it was too!'

Serves 4
4 pigeons
4 tablespoons butter
¼ cup flour
½ cup white wine
½ cup blanched white almonds
2 tablespoons lemon or lime juice
seasoning

Dust the birds in flour seasoned with salt and pepper. Melt the butter in a heavy skillet and sauté the pigeons until they are nicely browned. Add the wine and lemon/lime juice. Cover and simmer for 15–20 minutes, before adding the almonds and cooking for 5–10 minutes more or until the birds are 'fork' tender.

Boiled Pigeon

Like the recipe for Boiled Pike with Oysters (*see* page 155), this recipe is lifted directly from an old recipe book written by a lady named Hannah Wooley. Although I have included it exactly as written, it would be possible to update, adapt and use this particular recipe.

> Take your largest Pigeons and cut them in halves, wash them and dry them, then boil a little water and Salt with some whole Spice, and a little Faggot of sweet Herbs, then put in your pigeons and boil them, and when they are enough, take some boiled Parsley shred small, some sweet Butter, Claret Wine, and an Anchovy, heat them together, then put in the yolks of Eggs, and make it thick over the Fire, then put in your Pigeons into a Dish, garnished with pickled Barberries [fruit of the Barberry (*Berberis vulgaris*), which can also be used to make a type of jelly; if you have ever had *confitures d'epine vinette*, this is where the flavour comes from] and raw Parsley, and so pour over them your Sawce and serve it to the Table.
>
> (Taken from *The Queene Like Closet or Rich Cabinet*…; original publication date unknown.)

Hungarian Pigeon Soup with Pickled Gherkins and Soured Cream

This is more of a stew than a soup and is perfect for the winter – to make it even more substantial, try adding tinned butter beans or small dumplings.

Serves 6
225g/8oz pigeon breasts, minced
115g/4oz onion, chopped
340g/12oz potatoes, diced
225g/8oz tin tomatoes
850ml/1½pt stock
2 cloves garlic, peeled and crushed
4–6 pickled gherkins, sliced
30g/1oz butter
seasoning
soured cream

Fry the chopped onion and minced pigeon breasts in the butter until lightly browned. Add the diced potato and fry for a further 2–3 minutes. Stir in the canned tomatoes, the stock, seasoning and garlic. Simmer gently for 30 minutes; then add the sliced pickled gherkins. Heat for a further minute or so before ladling the soup into bowls and adding a swirl of soured cream. Serve with warm crusty bread and a glass or two of medium-heavy red wine.

Stuffed Pigeon

As with the Pigeon with Warmed Mushroom Salad, this recipe requires whole pigeons rather than merely using the breasts.

Serves 4

4 pigeons (retain their livers if the birds are being specially prepared for this dish)
4 tablespoons sausage meat
4 rashers streaky bacon
1 clove garlic, crushed
2 tablespoons white wine
1 tablespoon Cognac
1 tablespoon tomato purée
2 tablespoons olive oil
1 large slice stale white bread, broken into crumbs
1 tablespoon flour
2 eggs, beaten
2 sprigs parsley
nutmeg, grated
seasoning

Prepare the stuffing by mixing together the breadcrumbs, the crushed livers from the pigeons, sausage meat, garlic and sprigs of parsley. Add the eggs, nutmeg, seasoning, oil and Cognac and mix well for a second time before dividing the mixture and stuffing the insides of each bird. Put a rasher of bacon over the breasts of each bird. Place the pigeons in a casserole dish, sprinkle with the flour, moisten with the white wine, the tomato purée and about half a glass of water. Place in a moderate oven for around 45 minutes. Remove the birds and keep warm – they can be served whole, in halves or just the breasts – if choosing the latter method, remember to include a spoonful of the stuffing with each serving. De-glaze the casserole dish by adding a little more water or wine to the sauce residue, heat and stir until it is of a good consistency and pour over the birds before serving.

Guinea-Fowl and Quail

My time in Africa had left me bored with the prospect of guinea-fowl. However, this particular bird, reared by Edward's head gamekeeper, was quite a delight.

(J.E. Marriat-Ferguson, *Visiting Home*, 1905)

Guinea-Fowl are not native to the UK, but they are kept by many enthusiasts, and also oven-ready birds are easily sourced via supermarkets such as Waitrose. Most of these birds are bred in France rather than the UK – for some reason, French producers can supply birds much heavier than those produced at home and, as a result, several commercial breeders in the British Isles periodically introduce French-bred stock into their flocks.

There are several varieties of quail. Those produced commercially for meat in the UK have their origins in the Japanese or Corn quail, but, in the USA, Bobwhites are a regular quarry for many sportsmen and women. Both guinea-fowl and quail are readily available in the UK and, as their composition is identical to that of traditional game birds, it makes sense to include a least a few recipes.

Guinea-Fowl in Red Wine Sauce

Like the recipe for guinea-fowl in caramelized orange and pink peppercorn sauce, this recipe also involves pan-frying and finishing off in the oven, making them both possible to serve 35–45 minutes from start to finish. They both also involve alcohol, making it even better!

Serves 4
4 guinea-fowl breasts
170g/6oz streaky bacon, chopped
1 onion, peeled and chopped
225g/8oz button mushrooms
750ml/1¼pt stock
6 tablespoons brandy
350ml/12fl oz red wine
30g/1oz butter
1 tablespoon olive oil
4 tablespoons redcurrant jelly
seasoning

Melt the butter and oil in a frying pan; add the guinea-fowl and cook (skin-side down first) over a high heat for 3 minutes on each side. Transfer to an ovenproof dish and place in the oven at gas mark 2, 150°C/300°F.

Make the sauce by cooking the bacon, mushrooms and onion in the frying pan for about 5 minutes or until browned. Remove with a slotted spoon and set aside. Add the brandy, wine, stock and redcurrant jelly to the frying pan. Bring to the boil and cook for 15–20 minutes or until the sauce becomes thick and syrupy. Return the guinea-fowl breasts to the pan; bring to the boil and serve immediately. Serve with creamy mashed potatoes into which has been folded 2 tablespoons of very finely chopped chives.

Apple Creamed Guinea-Fowl
with Morel Mushrooms

Serves 4
2 guinea-fowl
12 thin rashers streaky bacon
1.1ltr/2pt game stock (*see* Chapter 15)
225g/8oz fresh morel mushrooms
55g/2oz butter
seasoning
Creamed Apple Sauce (*see* Chapter 15)

Remove the legs and wings from the guinea-fowl, place the birds in a saucepan and poach in stock for 10 minutes before removing and allowing to rest. Season the breasts and smear evenly with a thin layer of butter (use half the quantity given). Brown evenly in a frying pan before cooking in the oven at gas mark 6, 200°C/400°F for 5–10 minutes. Meanwhile, make the Creamed Apple Sauce; wash the mushrooms and sauté in the remaining butter and a little water. Grill the bacon until crisp. Take the guinea-fowl from the oven and remove the breasts, placing each in the centre of individual dining plates. Arrange the bacon rashers on top and spoon the morels around the side. Carefully pour the sauce over so as not to disturb the bacon and morels. Garnish with a few croutons and serve with game chips, French beans and apple sauce.

Guinea-Fowl in Caramelized Orange
and Pink Peppercorn Sauce

Serves 4
4 guinea-fowl breasts
For the sauce:
100g/3½oz sugar
zest and juice of 4 oranges
zest and juice of 1 lemon
3 tablespoons Cointreau liqueur
2 tablespoons cognac
2 tablespoons oil
55g/2oz pink peppercorns in brine (drained)
200ml/7fl oz game stock (*see* Chapter 15)

Guinea-fowl in caramelized orange and pink peppercorn sauce.

Deal with the simple part first! Pan-fry both sides of the guinea-fowl breasts in oil until golden brown, then transfer them to a low oven gas mark 4, 180°C/350°F for a further 30 minutes.

To make the sauce: place sugar, orange and lemon juice into a saucepan. Dissolve the sugar over a low heat and then turn up to the maximum in order to thicken the liquid and produce a light-coloured caramel. Add the zest, Cointreau, cognac, peppercorns and game stock. Still on a high flame, reduce the liquid until it is about ⅓ of its original quantity.

Remove the guinea-fowl breasts from the oven and leave to rest in a serving dish before adding the sauce over the top. Serve with either Parsnip and Apple Mash or Turnip and Tarragon Rôsti (*see* Chapter 14).

Sautéed Guinea-Fowl and Cabbage

This recipe is more tasty and interesting than the name and cooking method might suggest!

Serves 4
1 guinea-fowl, jointed into quarters
1 medium cabbage
4 tablespoons butter
1 teaspoon lightly crushed juniper berries
280ml/½pt double cream
¼ teaspoon paprika
seasoning

Brown the guinea-fowl joints in the butter. Cover the pan, lower the heat and leave to simmer for 15 minutes. Thinly slice the cabbage and blanch for a couple of minutes; drain and add to the guinea-fowl, together with seasoning and juniper berries. Cover and cook for a further 10 minutes before gently pouring in the cream and simmering with the lid off for 5 minutes. Sprinkle with the paprika just before serving with boiled potatoes.

Russian Guinea-Fowl

Serves 4
4 guinea-fowl breasts
115g/4oz button mushrooms, sliced
1½ tablespoons flour
140ml/¼pt stock
140ml/¼pt soured cream
3 tablespoons vodka
55g/2oz butter
paprika
seasoning

Fry the guinea-fowl breasts in the butter until cooked through. Transfer to a shallow ovenproof dish and keep them warm. Add the sliced mushrooms to the pan and fry until tender and turning golden. Spoon over the guinea-fowl breasts.

Stir the flour into the pan residue and then gradually blend in the stock. Stir over a hot heat until the mixture begins to reduce and a sauce consistency forms. Cool slightly before adding the soured cream. Mix in the vodka and seasoning, then pour over the breast meat. Garnish by dusting with paprika. Serve with buttered noodles, baby beets and green beans or a salad.

Creole Guinea-Fowl with Pineapple

Serves 4
1 guinea-fowl, jointed into four pieces
425g/15oz can pineapple slices, drained and cut into bite-sized chunks
4 celery stalks, cut into slices
3 spring onions, trimmed and chopped
2 green chillies, cut in half lengthways and de-seeded
1 banana, chopped and mashed
140ml/4fl oz stock
fresh coriander, finely chopped
Tabasco sauce
55g/2oz butter
large tin or carton coconut milk
seasoning

Melt the butter in a large pan, season the guinea-fowl pieces and fry for 10 minutes or until golden brown in colour. Remove from the pan with a slotted spoon and set to one side. Add the vegetables and pineapple to the pan and fry for 3 minutes or until softened and browned. Add the banana mash and return the guinea-fowl quarters to the pan; season again, at the same time adding a few drops of Tabasco sauce, together with most, but not all, of the chopped coriander. Pour the stock over, bring to the boil and then simmer for 30 minutes, or until the meat pieces are tender. Serve on a bed of rice that has been simmered in coconut milk rather than water, sprinkling the remainder of the coriander over the meat and sauce just before taking to the table.

QUAIL

For a dinner party one would probably need two birds per person or one each as a starter, but, roasted and served cold as an accompaniment to a summer salad or picnic, it perhaps cannot be bettered. In the opinion of many, quail meat is, like revenge, a dish best served cold! There are, however, some interesting hot dishes too.

French Quail Made Easy

Three quick recipes – all of which were at one time very popular in rural France.

Caille Papillons

Using scissors, cut each quail open down the length of its backbone. Open it; flatten it with a rolling pin or meat mallet (apparently the French housewives used their flat iron!). Cook it in butter in an ovenproof dish. It should be ready in 10 minutes.

Caille al la Crapaudine

Open a quail as above. Dip in flour, beaten egg and breadcrumbs in turn. Cook it in butter in a frying pan. Salt. Serve, pouring over it the butter from the pan, to which an extra knob has been added and rapidly melted.

Caille Rôsti

Brush the quail with melted butter before wrapping a rasher of bacon around each. Cook in a shallow roasting dish at gas mark 7, 220°C/450°F for 15–20 minutes, basting occasionally with more melted butter if necessary and the juices from the pan.

Cailles en Cocotte

Still keeping on a French theme, our neighbours offered me this recipe. I've not tried it, but it sounds simple and interesting.

Serves 4
4–8 quail
8 langoustines
55g/2oz each of diced carrot, red/green/yellow pepper and celery
225g/8oz fresh peas
1 chicken stock cube
1 tablespoon chervil, finely chopped
115g/4oz butter

Gently sweat the celery, carrots and pepper in butter for 5–10 minutes. In a flameproof casserole dish, poach the quail in the prepared chicken stock for around 20 minutes. Add the sweated vegetables, fresh peas and langoustines; cook for a further 10 minutes. Just before serving, add the butter juices from the pan in which the vegetables were sweated, together with the chervil.

Pan-Cooked Quail with Olives

Serves 4
4–8 quail
4 rashers streaky bacon, roughly chopped
12 olives, de-stoned
1 small onion, chopped
1 carrot, diced
425ml/¾pt stock
280ml/½pt dry white wine
2 tablespoons brandy
30g/1oz butter
½ teaspoon dried sage
seasoning

In a pan, heat the butter, season the birds and fry until browned. Put to one side and fry the bacon, onion and carrot in the same pan; once softened, remove from the heat and replace the quail.

In a small saucepan, heat the brandy over a gentle heat until it ignites; pour it immediately over the birds whilst still alight. Once the flames have died, add the stock, wine, sage and more seasoning before returning to the heat. Bring to the boil and then simmer gently for 15 minutes. Add the olives and cook for a further 10 minutes. Lift out the quail and keep warm; boil the pan contents until it reduces in volume by approximately half. Pour over the quail, which should, by now, be ready on a serving platter. Accompany with brown rice and a green salad.

Roast Quail with Noodles

Quick to cook but, for the best-tasting birds, they require marinating overnight. Use shop-bought noodles for speed of cooking.

4–8 quail
roasted pine nuts (for garnish)
a drizzle of either pine nut, walnut or hazelnut oil (to finish off)
For the marinade, mix together:
3 tablespoons soy sauce
3 tablespoons sherry
4 teaspoons oil
2 teaspoons sugar
2 teaspoons finely chopped shallot
2 teaspoons grated fresh ginger
1 level teaspoon salt

Coat the quail with the marinade, place them in a shallow dish and pour over any remaining mixture. Turn them occasionally and leave overnight in a cool place. Roast the birds as for Caille Rôsti (*see* above).

Cook the required amount of noodles as per the manufacturer's instructions. Drain well and make a 'noodle nest' in the centre of a serving dish. Place the roasted quail on top and drizzle with pine nut, walnut or hazelnut oil. Garnish with roasted pine nuts. Serve with a green salad, fried cabbage, or buttered steamed greens.

Quail Richelieu

As Melinda and I have a house in the town of Richelieu, Indre-et-Loire, France, I just had to include this recipe found in an old recipe book from the region. Interestingly, many recipes still advocate wrapping quail (and indeed partridge) in vine leaves.

Clean six tender young quail and truss the legs close to the body. Wrap the birds in grape leaves, then in large thin slices of fat pork and tie the larding securely with string. Heat a roasting dish in a very hot oven and lay the birds on their sides in the pan and roast them, basting often for five minutes and then turning the birds to roast them on their other side for five minutes more. At last, roast them on their backs for another five minutes. Discard the larding pork and string.

Remove the quail to another place and add a little water to the juices in the pan, cooking and stirring in the brown crustiness. Parboil three-quarters of a cup of carrots, celery and onion, cut in very fine uniform pieces, for two or three minutes. Drain the vegetables and cook until tender in three-quarters of a cup of veal stock. Stir in a *beurre manié* composed of butter kneaded with a little flour. Combine this with the quail juices and heat it well. Pour the sauce over the birds and simmer all together for four or five minutes longer.

(Translated from *Le livre des recettes gourmandes*, 1926)

Quail Tagine

A 'tagine' is a North African earthenware cooking pot. As Moroccan cookery quite often involves the use of many spices, I thought it appropriate to give this recipe a North African sounding name. If you happen to have brought a tagine home with you from holiday, it can be used to present the finished dish at the table.

Serves 4
4–8 quail, halved lengthways
3 onions
285g/10oz can chick beans or broad beans (with the outer skins removed)
115g/4oz dates, de-stoned
55g/2oz butter
1 tablespoon paprika
1 teaspoon saffron powder
½ teaspoon ground ginger
¼ teaspoon ground cinnamon
fresh sprigs of coriander and parsley
seasoning

Place the quail halves into a large heavy-based saucepan or flameproof casserole dish. Peel and chop one of the onions into thin rings and finely chop the other two. Add just the rings to the quail and also include the butter. Pour in just enough cold water to cover the quail pieces. Bring the pan slowly to the boil, reduce the heat and simmer for bout 30 minutes. Add the saffron, ginger, paprika, cinnamon, finely chopped onions, dates and chick beans (or broad beans) to the pan. Stir well, cover with tightly fitting lid and simmer for another 30 minutes.

Taste the liquid, season as appropriate and transfer all into a serving dish (or tagine). Roughly chop the coriander and parsley and sprinkle over. Serve with couscous and/or pitta bread.

QUAIL EGGS
Apart from using fresh eggs for hard-boiling as a picnic treat, another possibility is to hard boil them and place them in aspic or pickle them in vinegar and salt; or they can be smoked. The shell will dissolve completely if the boiled egg is placed in commercial vinegar for 12 hours, or it can be hand-peeled.

Potted Quail Eggs with Anchovy

Another interesting starter made from quail eggs. As many people dislike the idea of anchovy in any shape or form, the essence can be omitted. It does, however, lend a subtle taste to the dish. It may be kept refrigerated for storage but is best actually served at room temperature.

Serves 4–6
12 quail eggs, hard-boiled
170g/6oz butter
1 tablespoon onion, very finely chopped
4 tablespoons fresh single cream
1 tablespoon parsley, very finely chopped
3–4 teaspoons anchovy essence
seasoning

Gently melt the butter, add the onion and cook very carefully without colouring. Mash the eggs into a bowl and mix in the onion, melted butter and anchovy essence. Add the cream, seasoning and parsley. Turn the mixture either into individual small pots, such as ramekin dishes, or into one larger one. Smooth over the top, cover and chill until set. Serve the potted egg with crispy brown bread and watercress or crisp rye biscuits.

Curried Quail Eggs

If you have a ready supply of quails eggs and can be bothered to peel them after hard-boiling, this makes a wonderful savoury starter.

Serves 4
12–16 eggs, hard-boiled
30g/1oz butter
1 onion, skinned and chopped
2 teaspoons curry powder
30g/1oz flour
280ml/½pt milk
55g/2oz sultanas
55g/2oz cucumber, finely cubed
225g/8oz long-grained rice
salt and freshly ground black pepper

Boil the eggs, peel and keep warm in an ovenproof dish until required.

Melt the butter in a saucepan and fry the onion until soft, stir in the curry powder and flour and cook gently for 1 minute. Remove the pan from the heat and gradually stir in the milk. Bring back to the boil slowly and continue to cook, stirring all the while, until the sauce has thickened. Stir in the sultanas, cucumber and seasoning.

Cook the rice as per the manufacturer's instructions. Arrange around the quail eggs and pour the curry sauce over.

Scrambled Quail Eggs and Truffle

Halve the quantities for a romantic breakfast for two and serve with champagne.

Serves 4
24 quails eggs
55g/2oz butter
2 tablespoons double cream
55g/2oz black or white Alba truffle

Break the eggs into a bowl and add seasoning. Melt the butter in a pan without allowing it to burn and add the eggs, stirring all the time with a wooden spatula. Just as the eggs begin to scramble and solidify, stir in the double cream. Serve on white toasted and buttered bread, shaving thin slices of truffle over the eggs.

Rabbit and Hare

The broth of the hare: that's the best. The broth of the hare and the meat
of the rabbit. The meat of the hare is darker in colour; but the broth is the
best. Oh, the soup!… The soup and the broth is the best!
(John Connaughton, quoted by George Ewart Evans,
The Leaping Hare, 1972)

Rabbits and hares count as game, although only the hare is covered by the Ground Game Act of
1880. Without the humble rabbit, many countrymen would have fared far less well than they did in
times of poverty and war. Both have been the subject of illicit poaching for generations and it was
only when the viral disease myxomatosis began to appear in the 1950s, that rabbit meat began to be
eaten less regularly. It is, however, nowadays once more enjoyed by a great many people all the year
round with some claiming that a young, simply fried rabbit is the finest meal they know.

As is pointed out later in this section, hares and dishes made from them can be something of an
acquired taste, but on the off chance you get given one, we include a few suggestions you might like
to try. Generally most recipes suggest that both should be gently casseroled with vegetables, but
there are some interesting alternatives.

RABBIT

I would think that, after pigeon and pheasant, rabbits are the most commonly available 'country'
meat. Fortunately, there are many recipes available, making it possible to ring the changes. Most use
the same basic traditional British principles of sealing the meat, casseroling and slow cooking, but
some, such as the Paella Valenciana with Rabbit and the Rabbit Salmerejo have a little touch of
Spain about them.

Paella Valenciana with Rabbit

Serves 4
175g/6oz rabbit, chopped across the bone into 2cm/¾in pieces
450g/1lb pack seafood selection
boil-in-the bag mussels or fresh if possible
450g/1lb Calasparra or other good paella rice
2 tablespoons olive oil
1 onion, peeled and finely chopped
2 garlic cloves, finely chopped
1.5ltr/2½pt game or fish stock
1 big glass dry white wine
100g/3½oz tomato purée
a few *haricots verts*, chopped to 2cm/¾in slices
handful frozen peas
2 bay leaves
pinch paprika
pinch saffron
salt and freshly ground black pepper
30g/1oz parsley flakes or fresh chopped parsley
4–6 medium-sized cooked prawns for decoration
1 lemon, quartered

Heat the oil in a *paellera* (paella pan) or large frying pan over a low heat. Then add the onion and cook until softened and transparent; this will take approximately 5–8 minutes. (Avoid browning either the onion or the rice.) Prepare the mussels, then add the garlic, tomato purée, bay leaves and rabbit, and cook for a further 5–7 minutes or until the rabbit is cooked through.

Add the rice, paprika and saffron and mix to combine. Fry for 2–3 minutes then gradually add the stock, wine and *haricots verts*; bring to the boil and continue to cook for 2–3 minutes before reducing the heat to a gentle simmer and cooking for a further 18 minutes, stirring occasionally during the beginning of the cooking. Watch the paella does not boil dry, although it should be fairly dry at the end of the cooking time with perhaps a little moisture left in the bottom of the pan. Season to taste with a little salt and freshly ground black pepper.

Add the cooked seafood selection and frozen peas; push gently down into the rice and continue to cook for 2–3 minutes. Do not stir too much as this will fracture the rice. Add the mussels now, either boiled in bag or cooked separately. Fork them in very lightly. Remove the pan from the heat, cover with foil or more traditionally newspaper and leave to stand for 5 minutes – this is vital for good, fluffy rice. Finish with more parsley and lemon wedges to decorate. Add the cooked prawns round the edge then serve immediately – often to applause!

Rabbit in White Wine and Mustard

Serves 4–6
2 small rabbits, jointed
1 large onion, roughly chopped
1 clove garlic, crushed
1 stick celery, roughly chopped
1 leek, roughly chopped
bouquet garni
280ml/½pt dry white wine
1 tablespoon French mustard
1 dessertspoon double cream
flour
seasoning
pinch of thyme

Heat some oil and sauté vegetables and garlic before placing in a casserole dish. Put the flour into a polythene bag, add the rabbit joints and shake well until all the joints are coated. Remove and, in a frying pan, cook the rabbit until each joint is sealed, before transferring to casserole dish. De-glaze the frying pan with the wine and add to the casserole, together with the mustard, bouquet garni, thyme and seasoning. Cook at gas mark 4, 180°C/350°F for around 30 minutes. To serve, remove the rabbit pieces, reduce the sauce, add double cream and garnish with chopped flat-leaf parsley and croutons.

Lapin en Cidre

Living in France, I notice that almost every rural home still has its pen of rabbits outside the back door, that the weekend sportsmen around our home are never happier than when they've 'bagged' a rabbit, and that the meat sections of all the supermarkets always contain a good supply of rabbit meat. No wonder then, that the French have so many rabbit recipes, of which this is one.

Serves 4–6
2 rabbits, jointed
450g/1lb shallots
1ltr/1¾pt cider
225g/8oz breadcrumbs
3 sprigs thyme
2 bay leaves
2 juniper berries
1 teaspoon coriander seeds
1 teaspoon saffron

Heat a good 'glug' of olive oil in the bottom of a casserole dish and fry off the rabbit joints until they are sealed on all sides. Add the shallots, juniper berries, herbs and spices and cover with cider. Place the lid on the casserole and cook in the oven at gas mark 6, 200°C/400°F for around an hour before checking that the meat is still covered by liquid (top up with more cider if necessary) and lowering the oven temperature to gas mark 4, 180°C/350°F for another hour. Once cooked, transfer the rabbit joints to a warming plate and strain the casserole juices into a saucepan before adding the breadcrumbs and saffron, and bringing the temperature up to boil. Serve the resultant sauce poured over the rabbit pieces. Accompany with either boiled or minted and buttered new potatoes.

NB Traditionally, the French do not serve their main course with any vegetables other than potatoes.

Rabbit and Prunes

Marinade a jointed rabbit overnight in water to which vinegar has been added at the ratio of 1 teaspoon per 570ml/1pt water. Fry the rabbit pieces in 55g/2oz of butter until they are sealed. Remove from pan and fry 2 roughly chopped onions until they are soft and brown. Add 15g/½oz of flour to the pan and slowly add part of 425ml/¾pt of beer or cider until the mixture is smooth. Return the rabbit pieces to the pan, together with the remainder of the alcohol, a pinch of thyme, a bay leaf and seasoning. Bring to the boil and simmer for 30 minutes.

Add 225g/8oz stoned prunes to the pan and simmer for a further 30 minutes before serving with jacket potatoes and green beans.

Devilled Rabbit

Serves 4
1 rabbit, jointed
55g/2oz bacon, chopped
1 large onion, thinly sliced
280ml/½pt milk (just under)
4 tablespoons water
30g/1oz butter
30g/1oz flour
1 bay leaf
mustard
seasoning

Soak the rabbit joints in cold salted water overnight. Remove and dry before coating with mustard and seasoning. Place the joints in a casserole and add the bacon, onion, bay leaf and water. Cover and cook at gas mark 6, 200°C/400°F for an hour or until the rabbit is tender. Strain off the liquid from the casserole and make up to 280ml/½pt with milk.

In a small pan, melt the butter and slowly add the flour in order to make a roux. Gradually add the juice/milk liquid, bring to the boil and then simmer for 3 minutes, stirring continually.

Place the rabbit joints on a serving plate, cover with the thickened sauce and surround with either boiled long-grain rice or quenelles of mashed potato. For a vegetable, French beans and/or *petit pois* would go well. Alternatively, try steamed nettles! They taste just like spinach – pick them young, steam and serve with grated nutmeg over the top.

Steamed Stuffed Saddle of Rabbit with Nettle Mash

Talking of nettles as an accompaniment to rabbit!

Fry 225g/8oz mushrooms in a little butter, add a pinch of thyme and a little seasoning. Lay the 8 slices of streaky bacon on a sheet of cling film, place a boned saddle of rabbit on top, spoon the mushrooms across the centre and roll into a cylinder before tying the ends of the cling film in order to keep the shape. Steam the sausage-shaped parcel for 15–20 minutes.

Make a pan of mashed potatoes in the usual way, adding a good quantity of butter. Quickly steam young nettle leaves (removed from the stalks) in a pan containing a minimal amount of water. Chop and add to the potato mash. Alternatively, serve the nettles separately and add a squirt of proprietary nettle oil to the mash in order to give it a good rich colour.

Curried Rabbit

The addition of curry will obviously give this dish a very different flavour to the recipe for rabbit in white wine and mustard. The basic cooking methods are, however, very similar.

Serves 4
1 rabbit, jointed
2 large onions, chopped
1 large cooking apple, peeled, cored and chopped
570ml/1pt stock
30g/1oz butter
1½ tablespoons flour
1 tablespoon sultanas
1 tablespoon curry powder
1 teaspoon chutney
1 teaspoon redcurrant jelly
1 teaspoon oil
seasoning

Heat the butter and oil in a frying pan and fry the rabbit joints until golden, before transferring them to a casserole dish. Add the chopped onion to the pan and fry until soft, then sprinkle over the rabbit, together with the chopped apple. Put the curry powder and flour into the frying pan and fry for 2 minutes. Add the stock gradually and bring to the boil before incorporating all the remaining ingredients and pouring into the casserole. Cover and cook at gas mark 3, 170°C/325°F for 1½–2 hours. Serve on a bed of long-grained rice.

Rabbit Salmerejo

To get the authentic Spanish taste in this dish, it is well worth standing the rabbit joints overnight in a marinade made up of 280ml/½pt of dry white wine, 100ml/3fl oz of vinegar, 2 sprigs of fresh thyme, 2 tablespoons of fresh oregano and a bay leaf. Remember to reserve the marinade.

Serves 4

After removing the joints from the marinade, dry them thoroughly before browning them in a pan containing a little olive oil (do as the Spanish do and use the best quality oil available). Pour the marinade over, adding more wine if necessary to cover the rabbit pieces. Partially cover the pan and simmer gently. Meanwhile, crush 2 large cloves of garlic, 2 teaspoons of paprika, 1 small piece of hot red chilli pepper (or, alternatively, ½ teaspoon cayenne pepper) and a little salt with a pestle and mortar. Add to the pan, stir and continue cooking for approximately 1 hour or until the joints are tender. If the liquid looks in danger of 'disappearing', add more wine during cooking.

HARE

It would have been tempting to start this section with Mrs Beeton's oft-quoted saying, 'First catch your hare', but although it is often used, it is, in fact, not only misquoted, but also misattributed! The original *bon mot* began life as 'Take your hare when it is cased' and, according to *The Oxford Dictionary of Quotations*, it was not written by Mrs Beeton.

Having put the record straight on that one, there is much to be said about the hare in connection with game cookery. It has undoubtedly, very dark meat and older animals can have a very strong taste – both factors tend to put people off from trying it. An old Suffolk countryman once summed this attitude up in saying:

> I remember poaching hares in the early '20s, and the price that time would
> be about 7s. 6d. for a hare – much more than you got for a day's work. No,
> I don't like eating hare. In fact, I've never tried it. I think it's because of the
> meat; it's very dark, and there's a lot of blood: people don't like the blood
> and there's a smell that a lot of people don't like. The meat is very strong.

There is also the thought that, to make a hare 'tasty', a lot of ingredients need to be added and the purchase of these can make the dish quite expensive to prepare. In actual fact, most of what is required, such as onions, carrots, herbs and peppercorns, can all be found in the average larder, so don't be put off by any negative thoughts – unless that is, you are of a superstitious nature and believe, as many civilizations do, that the hare is a sacred animal and is associated with witchcraft!

A selection of pâtés and terrines made from rabbit and hare.

Terrine of Hare

900g/2lb pre-cooked hare meat, removed from the bones
900g/2lb pork
450g/1lb fat bacon pieces
1 packet bacon rashers
2 onions
1 wineglass brandy
parsley and thyme
salt and pepper

Blend or mince all the ingredients apart from the bacon rashers. Once everything is really well mixed, fill either one large or several small terrines with the mixture, put on top a couple of bay leaves and some rashers of bacon sliced and cut to fit. Cover the terrines with either greaseproof paper or kitchen foil and stand them in an ovenproof dish of water and cook in a slow oven for 1–2 hours, depending on the size of the terrines. Eat straight away once thoroughly cooled or store in the freezer for up to 3 months.

Hare Pâté

The actual quantities for this recipe are a little vague, as it depends upon the size of the hare – they do vary in size and weight in various parts of the country!

1 hare, jointed, but with the saddle removed
900g/2lb fat bacon off-cuts (bought very cheaply in most supermarkets), cubed
1 packet bacon rashers
3 onions, peeled and chopped
½ bottle red wine
stock
grated lemon peel
marjoram
1 bay leaf
seasoning

Place all the joints in a casserole dish, together with the onions, herbs and bacon. Add the wine and enough stock to cover the hare pieces. Place the lid on the casserole and cook in an oven at gas mark 4, 180°C/350°F for 45 minutes. (Lower the temperature if the meat looks to be cooking too quickly.) Let the dish cool, remove the hare meat and bacon, and push it through the fine plate of a mincer. Season well with ground black pepper, salt, a pinch or two of finely chopped herbs and a little grated lemon peel. Grease a 1.1ltr/2pt straight-sided terrine mould, but if you don't own such a thing, a straight-sided basin or ovenproof dish will do just as well.

Put the meat in the mould, but do not press it down too firmly. Lay a few rashers of bacon over the top and moisten with some of the juices in which you cooked the meat. Place greaseproof paper over the top and stand the mould in a pan or large bowl of boiling water. Put the pan/bowl and its contents into a low oven and cook for 1½–2 hours. Remove the mould from the pan and press down evenly on the greaseproof paper so that the meat consolidates. Leave the paper *in situ* while the pâté cools. In order to keep the pâté for longer (2–3 weeks if kept in the fridge), once the meat is cooled, run melted butter over the top and cover with tin foil.

This method should produce a tasty, coarse-grained pâté, which can be spread on toast, warm crusty bread or sliced and eaten with salad. The removed saddle could be used for Creamed Saddle of Hare (page 104).

Creamed Saddle of Hare

A saddle of hare will provide a meal for 4 people.

saddle of hare
30g/1oz butter
140ml/¼pt game stock
French mustard
For the marinade:
2 small onions, sliced
2 small carrots, sliced
280ml/½pt red wine vinegar
140ml/¼pt red wine
3 tablespoons oil
140ml/¼pt double cream
1 large sprig thyme
1 small sprig rosemary
2 bay leaves
6 peppercorns
salt

To prepare the marinade, heat the oil in a pan, add all the vegetables and cook slowly until soft. Add the remaining liquids and herbs, bring to the boil and simmer for 5 minutes. Pour into a large jug or bowl and leave to cool right down. Place the saddle of hare in the liquid and leave for 24 hours.

Smear the saddle with French mustard and melt 30g/1oz butter in a casserole in order to brown the saddle. Once this is done, strain the marinade, pour over the joint and simmer until the liquid has reduced by a third. Add 140ml/¼pt game stock and bring to the boil before covering the casserole and transferring it to the oven and cooking at gas mark 3, 170°C/325°F for 1–1½ hours or until the meat is tender. Remove the saddle from the casserole, reduce cooking juices over a low heat and add 140ml/¼pt cream before pouring over the saddle of hare. Serve with roast potatoes, braised onions or fennel and spinach.

Hare in a Sweet and Sour Sauce

Serves 4–6
1 hare, jointed
2½ tablespoons olive oil
4 tablespoons butter
6 rashers bacon, sliced (or *lardons*)
1 chopped onion
2–3 cups of game stock (*see* Chapter 15)
2½ tablespoons granulated sugar
½ cup white wine vinegar
4 tablespoons white raisins
4 tablespoons pine nuts
salt and pepper

Marinate the hare joints (*see* Chapter 15 for a suitable marinade) for at least 8 hours.

Heat the oil, butter and bacon together in a casserole dish and sauté the onion until soft. Remove the hare from the marinade, pat it dry with the aid of kitchen roll and dust well with flour before frying with the onion, oil and bacon. Strain about 2 cups of the marinade into the casserole and cook uncovered for 20 minutes over a medium heat until the marinade has reduced. Add salt and pepper and sufficient stock to cover the pieces of hare. Cover the casserole and simmer for a further 20 minutes. If after this time, the meat already seems cooked and yet the sauce is still watery, remove the hare joints and cook the sauce on a higher heat in order to reduce it.

In a pan, dissolve the sugar in 4 tablespoons of water. As it changes colour, add the vinegar, stirring constantly. Add the raisins and cook them for a few seconds until they begin to swell. Add this resultant sauce to the casserole, pouring it over the hare pieces, stir in the pine nuts and serve immediately on a bed of rice.

Hare and Dumplings

Serves 4
4 hare joints
115g/4oz streaky bacon rashers, chopped
4 sticks celery, chopped
2 leeks, trimmed, sliced
225g/8oz carrots, sliced
570ml/1pt game stock
2 tablespoons plain wholemeal flour
1 bay leaf
chopped chives
seasoning
basic dumpling mix (*see* page 207)

Fry the bacon in a flameproof casserole until the fat runs. Add the hare joints and fry until browned. Add the celery, leeks, carrots and bay leaf, mixing well. Sprinkle in the flour and stir in. Cook for 2 minutes before gradually adding the stock. Bring to the boil, stirring continuously and add seasoning. Cover and bake at gas mark 3, 160°C/325°F for 1½ hours or until the hare joints are tender.

Add a tablespoon of finely chopped chives to the basic dumpling mix, shape into rough balls and 20–25 minutes before cooking time is due to be completed, place them in the casserole. Cover and cook until the dumplings have risen and cooked through. Serve with mashed potatoes and runner beans.

Landlord's Hare

Serves 4–6

Tip 1 tablespoon of flour and 1 teaspoon of paprika (make sure you get the quantities the right way round!) into a strong polythene bag. Add all the joints of a small young hare and shake well to ensure that all the meat is well covered with the flour/paprika mix. Heat 55g/2oz of dripping in a flameproof casserole and fry the hare joints until browned on all sides. Add a clove of crushed garlic, 2 medium onions, each stuck with 2, cloves and 570ml/1pt of brown ale. Bring to the boil, cover tightly and place in an oven set at gas mark 2, 150°C/300°F for 3–4 hours or until the meat comes off the bone. Remove the onions. In a bowl, add a few spoonfuls of gravy to the blood of the hare (this gives a rich glossiness to the sauce, which is otherwise unobtainable); mix well and pour back into the casserole. Add 1 wineglass of port, and heat gently without boiling. Serve with mashed or boiled potatoes, broccoli and redcurrant jelly – the latter being the traditional accompaniment to all hare recipes.

NB If you are given or buy a hare frozen, you will not have its blood, in which case, thicken the liquid by mashing together a combination of 55g/2oz soft butter and 4 teaspoons of flour. When this is a smooth paste, add it to the liquid and stir until it boils.

Italian Hare

Carolyn Little includes this recipe in her book, *The Game Book* (Crowood, 1988). The addition of chocolate might make it suitable for the country writer, Duff Hart-Davis (*see* Chapter 12).

Serves 4

Soak a young, jointed hare for 1 hour in water to which a tablespoon of vinegar has been added, and prepare a stock by boiling the hare's liver in 280ml/½pt water.

Next, make a marinade consisting of 1 chopped onion, the liver stock, 280ml/½pt red wine and a bay leaf. Remove the hare joints from the water, pat them dry and place them in the marinade for 5 hours. Remove; strain the marinade and put to one side.

Begin making a sauce by preparing:

2 onions, cut into rings

3 tablespoons olive oil and 30g/1oz butter

30g/1oz flour

115/4oz piece of cooked ham, diced

55g/2oz raisins

30g/1oz flaked almonds

85g/3oz plain chocolate

salt and pepper

Fry the onion rings in half the oil until they are tender. Remove from the pan, heat the remaining oil and butter in the same pan, coat the hare joints with the flour and fry them gently until golden brown. Gradually add the marinade to the pan, stirring as it comes to the boil and thickens. Add the ham and cover the pan. Simmer for 1½ hours or until the meat is tender – add more stock as necessary.

Stir in the onions, raisins, almonds and chocolate, season to taste and heat gently for a further 10 minutes. Place the hare on a large dish of buttered green noodles and spoon the sauce over.

Venison and Wild Boar

For every beat there should be a stalker, two gillies, and at least two strong hill ponies to bring home the deer. There should be a large and airy larder, weighing scales and haunch boxes.

(Francis Ogilvy, *The 'House' on Sport*, 1899)

There are many things one can do with all cuts of venison: the shin, for instance, sliced into small pieces, can be treated exactly as a shin of veal; stews and casseroles can be made from cuts that traditionally require long, slow cooking; and the meat can also be easily adapted for established recipes such as suet puddings. Roasting can, however, sometimes lead to disappointment, due to the fact that venison is such a lean meat. Judging the cooking time for a joint of venison largely depends on the particular joint and, to some extent, what type of deer the meat comes from. Red and fallow can be very rare in the manner of roast beef, but roe should possibly be cooked a little more like lamb. Of course there is no reason why any joint shouldn't be 'well done' if that's how you prefer it.

COOKING GUIDELINES

As a general guide however, the following 'rules' apply:

- The haunch and saddle are the classic cuts for roasting, but bone-rolled shoulder is cheaper to buy.
- Before cooking, evaluate the particular joint and take into account its size, shape and density. If there is a bone running through it, this will conduct heat to the centre more quickly. For heavily boned joints, it may be necessary to almost double the cooking time.
- To serve a roast pink, brush with oil and brown it first, and cook at a higher temperature for slightly less time than recommended. To serve well done, make deep slits in the joint and press in fat and garlic. Again, brown all over, but cook covered at a lower temperature for a longer period.
- For a 1.35–2.7kg/3–6lb joint of venison: cook at gas mark 9, 240°C/475°F for the first 15–20 minutes before reducing the temperature to around gas mark 5, 190°C/375°F for the remainder. Once cooked, remove and rest the joint for 20 minutes, either in a food warmer or oven set below 75°C/170°F.

- Allow 30 minutes per 450g/1lb for a 1.8kg/4lb saddle of roe; 40 minutes for the same weight saddle of fallow. For a haunch of roe or fallow, allow 1¼–1½ hours for a 2.25kg/5lb joint.
- Test the meat as it cooks – a spongy texture means it is still underdone, as the meat becomes more resistant to the touch the more it cooks.
- Surround the joint with chopped root vegetables and add red wine or vegetable stock to help retain moisture.
- Basting frequently with port or another liquid will add moisture and flavour and act as the basis for the gravy.

Venison Liver

Fresh venison liver is, to my mind, the best and simplest of meals.

Serves 4
450g/1lb deer liver
4 red onions, peeled and chopped
115g/4oz butter
brandy or sherry
double cream
seasoning

Soften the red onions in butter. Fry the liver on either side and take out of the pan when cooked. Add a good 'glug' of brandy or sherry to the pan and season well with sea salt and black pepper. Once the sauce is bubbling, place the liver back in the pan and cook for a minute. Stir in a little double cream before serving.

The following is an interesting alternative to the above and also serves 4:

450g/1lb liver
115g/4oz button mushrooms
115g/4oz tomatoes, skinned
1 eating apple, sliced
sage, chopped
root ginger, grated
2 teaspoons garlic purée
2 teaspoons soy sauce
1 teaspoon coarse grain mustard

In a lightly oiled frying pan blend together the mushrooms, tomatoes, sage, garlic, apple, mustard, ginger and soy sauce before adding the liver and cooking until the pieces are cooked but the insides are still slightly pink.

Deer Kidneys in a Batter Bed

Serves 4
8–12 kidneys, skinned, cored and chopped
1 large onion, peeled and chopped
1 clove garlic, crushed
340g/12oz mushrooms, finely chopped
2 glasses dry sherry
85g/3oz butter
140ml/¼pt double cream
280ml/½pt milk
225g/8oz flour
2 eggs
seasoning

Sieve the flour and salt. Gradually beat in the eggs and add the milk gradually. Whisk until smooth and leave to stand. Sauté the kidneys and onion in 55g/2oz of butter until the onion is soft but not browned; add the mushrooms, garlic and sherry before cooking gently for a few minutes and then adding the cream. Simmer until the sauce is reduced and thickened.

Heat the remaining 30g/1oz butter in a flan dish, add the batter and spoon the kidney mixture into the middle. Bake at gas mark 6, 200°C/400°F for 30–35 minutes or until the batter pastry is crisp, golden and well risen. Cut and serve immediately.

Creamed Venison Sweetbreads

Definitely a recipe for the enthusiastic stalker who can, quite literally, get his hands on the main ingredients, but not one for the more squeamish gastronome!

Serves 4
12 deer sweetbreads
225g/8oz mushrooms, sliced
280ml/½pt dry white wine
140ml/¼pt double cream
55g/2oz butter
45g/1½oz plain flour
1 onion, finely chopped
salt and pepper

Melt the butter in a pan, add the sweetbreads and onion and cook for 5 minutes. Introduce the mushrooms and cook for a further 5 minutes before stirring in the flour and cooking for 1–2 minutes. Add the wine and seasoning and cook for another 5 minutes. At the last minute, add the cream, taking care that it does not separate, and serve on a bed of boiled rice accompanied by a mixed salad or selection of vegetables.

Venison and Wild Mushrooms

Serves 4
450g/1lb thick venison steak, cut into large chunks
30g/1oz dried porcini mushrooms
1 onion, finely chopped
2 garlic cloves, skinned and thinly sliced
12 juniper berries
seasoned flour
2 wineglasses red wine
280ml/½pt strong game stock
thyme leaves
olive oil
seasoning

Place the porcini mushrooms in a bowl and cover with warm water. Leave to soak and swell. Place the seasoned flour in a polythene bag, add the venison pieces and shake in order to coat well. Heat 2 tablespoons olive oil in a pan and gently fry the onion and garlic until they are soft but not discoloured. Increase the heat, add the venison chunks and cook until all the sides are browned. Use a pestle and mortar to crush the juniper berries and add them to the meat before adding the red wine, stock and strained porcini liquid. Bring to the boil and then add the chopped porcini and thyme leaves. Season and simmer until the meat is tender and the sauce is reduced and thickened. Serve heaped on top of a 'nest' of mashed potato at the centre of individual dinner plates, together with a selection of green vegetables.

Venison with Fresh Pear Chutney

This is a recipe from the wonderfully successful 'Game's On' campaign, which, along with 'Game-to-Eat', aims to support and promote the supply of local, healthy seasonal food and increase the amount of game sold through supermarkets.

Serves 4
900g/2lb venison fillet or boned leg
1 teaspoon thyme
1 bay leaf
olive oil
salt and pepper

Roll and tie the meat with butcher's string. Mix together the herbs and pepper and rub into the meat. In a flameproof casserole, heat the olive oil and seal the meat on all sides before seasoning with salt and roasting at gas mark 4, 180°C/350°F for 20 minutes.

Make the pear chutney by peeling, coring and roughly chopping 2 pears. Put these, together with 1 small chilli (de-seeded and chopped), 1 crushed clove of garlic, 1 grated small piece of ginger, a cinnamon stick, pinch of ground cloves, 55g/2oz granulated sugar and 2 tablespoons of apple cider vinegar, into a small pan and cook gently until the sugar has dissolved. Simmer until the pears are soft (about 15 minutes).

Venison with fresh pear chutney.

Parsley-Breaded Rack of Venison with a Blackcurrant Sauce

Serves 4

Make the parsley-breaded 'crust' that will eventually cover the top of an 8-bone rack of venison, by placing, in a food processor, 115g/4oz fresh white breadcrumbs, 45g/1½oz Cheddar cheese, 30g/1oz chopped fresh parsley and 55g/2oz softened butter. Blend to a dough consistency and roll out between two sheets of baking parchment until it is large enough to cover the top of the venison. Leave to rest in the fridge until required.

Next, season the meat and place a roasting tin over a high heat until very hot. Add a tablespoon of oil and seal the venison on all sides. Remove the pan from the heat, cover the meat with the bread crust and place in the oven at gas mark 4, 180°C/350°F for 20 minutes. Remove the rack of venison from the oven and allow to rest in a warm place for about 10 minutes. Carve by allowing two cutlets per person.

Make a blackcurrant sauce by melting 30g/1oz of butter and sweating 2 peeled and chopped shallots until soft. Add 55ml/2fl oz Cassis liqueur, turn up the heat and reduce until the mixture is almost dry. Then add 400ml/14fl oz beef stock and simmer until the sauce reduces by about a third. At this stage, introduce 115g/4oz of blackcurrants to the sauce and continue cooking until they are warmed through. Spoon the sauce around the cutlets and serve with a mixed swede and carrot mash, together with steamed spinach.

Parcelled Venison Steaks

Serves 4
4 loin or haunch steaks; cut about 1–2cm (½–¾in) thick
30g/1oz butter
1 medium onion, skinned and finely chopped
225g/8oz mushrooms, wiped and sliced
115ml/4fl oz red wine
115ml/4fl oz soured cream or yoghurt
2 tablespoons lemon juice
seasoning

Marinade the steaks for 24 hours, using a combination of ingredients from the suggestions made in Chapter 15.

Melt the butter in a large frying pan and seal the venison steaks well, keeping them flat by pressing firmly down with the blade of the spatula. Remove from the pan and place each on individual squares of foil cut about 20cm (8in) square.

Add the onions and mushrooms to the butter remaining in the pan and cook for 5 minutes. Stir in the red wine and the lemon juice and bring to the boil. Reduce the liquid by half, then remove from the heat and stir in the soured cream or yoghurt. Season well.

Place a quarter of the mushroom mixture on top of each steak, then shape the foil into parcels, sealing well. Put the parcels into a shallow ovenproof dish and bake in the oven at gas mark 4, 180°C/350°F for 30–40 minutes, until the steaks are tender. To serve, place each parcel on a plate and take sealed to the table, allowing your guests to open their own. Accompany with small new potatoes, boiled in their jackets and sautéed in butter, together with green beans.

WILD BOAR

Mary I (Bloody Mary), Queen of England, Wales and Ireland and the eldest daughter of Henry VIII was reputed to be 'particularly fond of wild boar meat'. At that time, the boar's head was considered to be quite a delicacy and, because of the interest in hunting, the wild boar survived in England up until the seventeenth century. Without the patronage of royalty and noblemen, natural stocks of wild boar would probably have died out long before then due to its tendency to destroy the crops being grown in newly felled areas of woodland.

Boar meat is once again becoming readily available in the UK, both from the ever-increasing feral numbers and as a result of being farmed as alternative meat.

CURING BOAR HAMS

Cured hams are a countrywide tradition, with many regions specializing in its own cure. The ingredients are many and varied, ranging from salt through to treacle and sugar. Used mainly in the past by country dwellers as a means of preserving the cottage pig, curing is nevertheless an interesting way of producing a wild boar ham that tastes divine – no wonder that such joints are popular in French supermarkets around Christmas-time.

Equipment

All that is really required is a large, smooth, wooden or marble work surface and a plastic bowl in which the meat can be immersed. A cool place equipped with a few hooks from which to hang the hams and a supply of muslin to protect them from flies and dust are essential, but other than that, not much more is needed other than time and effort.

Smoking after curing is a little more difficult. You may be able to get the joints done professionally or even build your own smoker (which is, of course, outside the remit of this particular book), but the old methods involved open hearths, dry and damp straw, oak shavings, juniper berries, various herbs and a process as like as not to set the building alight!

Curing Recipes

Either leg or shoulder of boar may be used, but whichever is chosen, it must be freshly killed. The following recipes assume a joint size of 7.25kg/16lb.

Beer Curing

450g/1lb soft brown sugar
450g/1lb 'common' or block kitchen salt
15g/½oz 'bay' or 'Maldon' salt
15g/½oz saltpetre
115g/4oz juniper berries
1.7ltr/3pt beer

Put all the ingredients into a saucepan and bring to the boil. Leave until cold before pouring over the ham. Rub every day for the first week, turning the joint thoroughly in the mixture, then every 2 days for a month. Remove from the mixture and hang to dry.

Sweet Curing

1.1ltr/2pt beer
1.1ltr/2pt vinegar
1.1ltr/2pt water
450g/1lb granulated sugar
450g/1lb 'bay' or 'Maldon' salt
450g/1lb kitchen salt
55g/2oz hops
15g/½oz peppercorns
15g½oz saltpetre
15g/½oz cloves

Boil together the beer, sugar, bay salt, peppercorns, vinegar, saltpetre, salt and cloves. Also boil the hops in the water for 30 minutes before straining the hop liquid and adding to the beer liquor. When cold, pour over meat joint placed in shallow container. Baste the joint with liquid every day and hang to dry after 6 weeks.

Curly Kale with Wild Boar Pancetta and Pecan Nuts

This serves 4 as a side dish – double the quantities for a more fulfilling summer lunch.

Heat a large frying pan and toast 55g/2oz shelled pecans, stirring for 5 minutes or until they colour slightly and begin to give off a nutty aroma. Remove the nuts from the pan; add 1 tablespoon of olive oil and 85g/3oz of wild boar pancetta and fry for 2–3minutes or until brown. Add 2 peeled and thinly sliced garlic cloves and half a chopped and de-seeded red chilli. Cook on a high heat for only 30–60 seconds and, when the garlic looks brown, tip 225g/8oz of curly kale into the pan and season with salt. Stir-fry for 3–4 minutes, or until the kale has just wilted and is tender. Throw in the toasted pecans and serve.

Braised Boar and Beetroot

Beetroot has a tenderizing effect on any meat – it apparently contains the same enzyme as papaya, which is used specifically as a meat tenderizer.

Serves 6–8
1.35kg/3lb wild boar; cut into cubes about 2.5cm/1in
3 medium onions, skinned and finely sliced
2 cloves garlic, skinned and finely chopped
3 uncooked beetroot, peeled and sliced into thin strips
850ml/1½pt game stock
140ml/¼pt port
140ml/¼pt crème fraîche
2 tablespoons flour
4 tablespoons oil
55g/2oz butter
seasoning

Place the flour and seasoning into a large polythene bag, add the cubes of boar meat and shake well until all the pieces are well covered. Heat the oil and butter in a heavy casserole and brown the boar meat on all sides, remove and put to one side. In the same casserole, cook the onions until they are soft and just beginning to change colour. Then add the garlic and beetroot strips and cook for 5 minutes, stirring occasionally. Add in the stock and port, stirring until the liquid begins to bubble. Return the boar pieces to the casserole and cover.

Cook in the oven at gas mark 4, 180°C/350°F for 1½ hours. Serve with a spoonful of crème fraîche on each serving and accompany with either jacket or mashed potatoes and stir-fried cabbage, into which 2 teaspoons of coarse-grained mustard has been added.

Wild Boar Pancetta and Onion Ciabatta

Another recipe that makes good use of wild boar pancetta is this one. It makes three loaves and is a great idea for picnics.

400g/14oz wild boar pancetta
400g/14oz onion
40g/1¼oz yeast
1.2ltr/2½pt water
2kg/4lb 7oz strong white flour
55g/2oz salt
butter

Wild boar pancetta and onion ciabatta.

Place the yeast in a bowl with half the quantity of water and mix together gently for a few seconds before leaving it to ferment at room temperature for about 10 minutes.

Slice the onion and pancetta into strips before frying each separately in a knob of butter. Once cooked, put them to one side.

When the yeast mix appears frothy, add the flour and the remaining water. Mix in a food processor at a slow speed for around 2 minutes until a dough is created. Add the salt to the dough and then mix on medium speed for a further 10 minutes, after which time it should be soft and pliable, but not sticky. Mix in the previously prepared boar pancetta and onions until both ingredients are thoroughly incorporated.

Take the dough from the bowl and cut it into three loaves: knead and fold each loaf into itself until the texture becomes elastic. Place the loaves on a tray and cover each with tea towels that have been lightly coated with flour, before leaving to 'prove' in a warm place. They should approximately double in size.

Preheat the oven to gas mark 9, 250°C/400°F and spray a little water onto the oven sides in order to create steam. Dust the top of each loaf with flour and cut three grooves across each one. Place them on a lightly floured baking tray and bake for 20 minutes before turning down the oven to around gas mark 6, 200°C/400°F and baking for a further 20 minutes until they are golden brown in colour.

Boar Chops Baked in Cream

Serves 4
4 good-sized wild boar chops (or any suitably-sized cut)
3 onions, skinned and thinly sliced
280ml/½pt beef stock
280ml/½pt double cream
2 tablespoons brandy
1 tablespoon curry powder
1 tablespoon plain flour
1 tablespoon sunflower oil
55g/2oz butter
seasoning

Heat the butter and oil together in a flameproof casserole dish and brown the boar chops on each side, removing to a warm dish as they brown. Add the sliced onions to the pan and cook until they are soft and beginning to colour. Stir in the curry powder and the flour, cooking for 1 minute before, gradually and very gently, stirring in the stock and cream. Season and add the brandy. Let the sauce bubble and then replace the chops, pushing them right into the sauce. Bake in the oven at gas mark 4, 180°C/350°F for 10–15 minutes. Serve with diced potatoes and lightly steamed sugar-snap peas.

Wild Boar Casserole with Beer

Serves 4
900g/2lb boar meat, cubed into 3cm/1½in pieces; remove any gristle and sinew
2 onions, peeled and roughly chopped
2 garlic cloves, peeled and crushed
285ml/10fl oz game stock
285ml/10fl oz brown ale
1–2 bay leaves
2 sprigs thyme
1 tablespoon flour
2 teaspoons light brown sugar
2 tablespoons oil
freshly ground black pepper

Fry the boar cubes in oil in a flameproof casserole dish until browned and sealed on all sides, adding more oil as required. Transfer to a plate with a slotted spoon. Add the onions to the casserole and fry for 3–5 minutes until lightly browned. Return the meat to the pan and add the garlic and stir in the flour. Gradually stir in the stock and brown ale, all the time scraping up any juices stuck to the bottom of the pan. Simmer and add the sugar, bay leaves and thyme and season with the black pepper. Cover tightly and cook in the oven at gas mark 2, 150°C/300°F for at least 2 hours or until the meat is tender. Serve with rice, roasted carrots and a creamy purée of celeriac.

COOKED BOAR HAM

Finally in this section, there is perhaps, nothing to beat a simply cooked or boiled wild boar joint. It may be cooked in either water or cider. When a joint is to be glazed, it is usual to first boil the meat before cooking in the oven.

Boiling

Soak the meat overnight in water, then place into a saucepan of cold water to which has been added a tablespoon of sugar and a bay leaf. Bring to the boil, cover and simmer, allowing a cooking time of 25 minutes per 450g/1lb and 25 minutes over. If the joint is left to cool in the cooking water, it will help retain the flavour and also make it easier to carve. Remove the skin before serving.

Glazing

Score the fat in large diamond shapes and stick a clove in each diamond, sprinkle liberally with brown sugar and cook at an oven temperature of gas mark 6, 200°C/400°F for 20 minutes. For that extra touch, baste occasionally with cider during cooking.

Oven Cook

To oven cook from start to finish, soak the joint in water for 24 hours; drain thoroughly and wrap in foil. Bake at gas mark 4, 180°C/350°F for 15 minutes per 450g/1lb, allowing an extra 15 minutes. At 20 minutes before the end of cooking time, remove the foil and skin and cut the fat into diamonds as before. Again, spike each diamond with a clove, cover with brown sugar and return to the oven to finish, remembering to baste with cider.

Game and Fish Pies

Still, Christmas was Christmas all the world over and even amongst the poorest, so she had managed to make the couple of rabbits, the Earl of Ashton's Christmas-box, into a most gorgeous pie for the morrow's dinner…

(A.G. Street, *The Gentleman of the Party*, 1936)

Game and fish pies make excellent winter dishes when served piping hot after a day out in the countryside. They are tasty and filling, giving the diner that all-important feel-good factor, especially when accompanied by a bottle of good red wine and followed by a contemplative doze in front of a roaring log fire! Some game pies, however, need not be reserved for the winter months: the best I ever tasted was served to me at the back of one of the Game Fair's hospitality tents on a scorching July day and cold game pies can form the basis of any good picnic, no matter what the season.

Mrs Beeton included joints of roast and boiled beef, shoulders of lamb, a variety of poultry, lobsters and pies in her outdoor eating suggestions. She also suggested ale, ginger beer, sherry, claret, champagne and brandy. Whilst that might be a little over-the-top for the local point-to-point or average shoot lunch, the inclusion of some sort of cold pie is always a good idea. Before thinking about a suitable filling, it is necessary to have a little understanding of what types of pastry are the most appropriate.

PASTRY

The trick with pastry making, as no doubt your Granny will have told you, is to work with cold hands, which will help prevent the dough from sticking to your fingers. If your hands are warm, periodically hold them under the cold tap, drying thoroughly before continuing. When making puff or flaky pastry, if the butter begins breaking through the pastry, or the pastry is becoming warm, stop, wrap and chill it for at least 30 minutes. Always work on a floured board and with a floured rolling pin. Once a batch of pastry is made up, it can be kept in the fridge for a couple of days or even frozen until such time as it is needed.

Basic pastry dough mixes can be enhanced by the addition of toasted ground spices, chopped fresh herbs or toasted and finely chopped nuts, which should only be added immediately prior to use.

Quiches and Tarts

The secret to baking a perfect quiche or tart is to pre-cook the pastry before adding the filling – attempting to cook both together, especially when a tart is egg-based, will only result in either partially raw pastry or curdled and over-cooked eggs. Even tarts with a non-eggy filling will benefit from pre-baking, as that way the heat can penetrate the pastry without the risk of it being 'insulated' by the chosen filling. Brushing the resulting hot pastry with egg white (*see* Shortcrust Pastry below) before adding the filling and cooking further will help in negating the possibility of the pastry ending up with a soggy base. To prevent pastry from becoming crumbly and difficult to handle, don't over-mix or add insufficient amounts of liquid. It is also important to weigh ingredients carefully and handle the dough gently.

Blind Baking

The traditional method of blind baking involves covering the pastry with a sheet of greaseproof paper and filling it with either real or ceramic baking beans – both of which are poor conductors of heat and therefore prevent the pastry base from cooking unevenly. Far better is the practice of using a sheet of kitchen foil, cut as long as the circumference of the baking tin. Line the tin with pastry and roll the foil into a long thin strip before coiling it firmly around inside the pastry, pressing it firmly against the sides to make an inner ring. Doing so helps in keeping the sides of the pastry case rigid whilst still allowing unhindered access by the heat.

To bake, pre-heat the oven to gas mark 6, 200°C/400°F and cook for 10–15 minutes until the pastry is dry and just beginning to colour. Remove the foil and check for any cracks that may allow the filling to escape. Patch these up with a piece of left-over pastry (returning the base to the oven for a further 5 minutes), but do not worry about any inconsequential cracks. Use a pastry brush and the egg white left over from making the pastry to coat the whole of the inside of the pastry case – the residual heat will bake it onto the pastry, thus sealing it immediately.

Shortcrust Pastry

The following recipe provides just enough pastry to thinly line a 20cm/8in tin:

115g/4oz plain flour
55g/2oz cold butter
pinch of salt
1 egg, separated

Rub the butter into the flour and salt until it resembles fine breadcrumbs (use a food processor if you prefer). Next, mix the egg yolk with a tablespoon of cold water and add to the flour and butter mixture, using your hands to draw the mixture together. If the mixture is too dry, sprinkle a little water, if it's too sticky, sieve in a little extra flour. Make a ball of the mixture, kneading it lightly to make it smooth. Flatten the ball into a disc, wrap in cling film and chill for half an hour. Save the egg white for the baking (*see* notes above).

Shortcrust is a good all-purpose pastry that is relatively easy to handle. To make rich game pies, picnic pasties and the like, the addition of extra fats is recommended. The following will make 350g/12oz of pastry. For larger amounts double up the quantities, but the important thing to remember are the proportions of half fat to flour, with enough liquid to combine. If you don't wish to use lard, substitute a white vegetable fat.

225g/8oz plain flour
55g/2oz butter
55g/2oz lard
pinch of salt

Mix the flour and salt in a bowl. Cut the fat into cubes and rub this into the flour until the mixture resembles fine breadcrumbs. Begin adding a total of 2–3 tablespoons of water very slowly, stirring it in with a knife. When the pastry is at the point where it just binds together, knead it lightly until it forms a ball. As in the previous recipe for shortcrust, wrap it in cling film and chill in the fridge for about half an hour before use.

Flaky Pastry

This is really a cheat's version because it doesn't involve the turning, rolling and resting. The secret is in the use of frozen grated butter, thus avoiding the need for tedious rubbing-in. All you need to remember is that the dough should come together in such a way that it leaves the bowl fairly clean, with no bits of loose butter or flour anywhere. Makes approximately 500g/1lb 2oz:

285g/10oz plain flour
285g/10oz unsalted butter, frozen and grated
1 egg
pinch of salt

Sift the flour into a large mixing bowl and stir in the salt. Toss the grated butter into the flour with clean hands. Cut the butter into the flour with a fork, so that it is well distributed. Make a well in the centre of the flour. Whisk the egg and 3 tablespoons of iced water together and pour it into the well in the flour. Add to the dry ingredients and, using a fork or metal spoon, stir in the egg mixture until you have a crumb-like dough. With floured fingers, draw the mixture together to make a dough in the bowl. Turn out the pastry onto a lightly floured work top and knead two or three times so that it is smooth (don't over-work the dough). Wrap the pastry in cling film and refrigerate it for at least 30 minutes.

Rough Puff Pastry

Compared to the flaky and puff pastry, this is easier to make and is ideal for rich pies such as game and venison. Makes approximately 450g/1lb:

225g/8oz plain flour
115g/4oz butter
115/4oz lard
1 teaspoon lemon juice
pinch of salt

Mix together the flour and salt. Cut the fats into cubes and mix it into the flour without breaking up the lumps. Add approximately 100ml/3½fl oz cold water together with the lemon juice and form into a stiff dough. Using a floured board, roll the dough into a strip three times as long as it is wide, before folding the top third down and the bottom third up. Turn the pastry sideways and seal the edges. Continue to roll and fold in a similar fashion until you have done it four times – although it is obviously more time-consuming, better results are obtained if you leave the pastry to rest between each session of rolling and folding. Chill in the fridge for half an hour before using.

Hot-Water Crust Pastry

Hot-water crust pastry is the traditional way of making game pies and was the favoured pastry of the Victorian and Edwardian era. For a rather special pastry of this nature, *see* Chapter 14 and the Hand-Raised Grouse and Foie Gras Pie with Apricot and Wild Mushrooms, as made at Claridge's, London. The following pastry is, however, a good general-purpose alternative:

225g/8oz plain flour
55g/2oz lard
55g/2oz butter
1 egg
60ml/2fl oz water
1 teaspoon salt

Place the lard, butter and water in a saucepan. Heat gently until melted, but not boiling.

Put the flour and salt in a mixing bowl. Make a dip in the centre and add the beaten egg, stirring it gently around with a knife so it is mixed with the flour. Pour in the melted fat and water mixture. Knead lightly to get a dough, adding a little more flour if it is too sticky to handle or a little more water if still too crumbly.

Wrap the pastry in cling film and chill for 45 minutes. Use as required, making sure you keep it covered when not in use.

Cheese Pastry

There are some recipes that may benefit from the addition of an extra savoury taste to the pastry. Flaked pheasant breast pieces, for example, are given an extra dimension when baked in a cheese pastry and served cold; they make good picnic food. Makes 250g/9oz:

140g/5oz flour
85g/3oz butter or margarine
30g/1oz mature Cheddar, finely grated
1 tablespoon freshly grated Parmesan

Place the flour and pepper seasoning into a bowl. Cut up the butter or margarine into cubes and rub them into the flour with your fingertips. Keep rubbing in the butter until there are no traces of fat left. Add the very finely grated cheeses and a tablespoon or two of iced water. Work the dough into a ball with your hands and knead it very gently to get it to a consistent mix.

Suet Pastry

Turn a game casserole into a Hob-Cooked Hot Game Pie by the inclusion of a suet pastry crust made as follows:

115g/4oz plain flour
60g/2oz suet, grated
¼ teaspoon baking powder
pinch of salt

Combine the flour, suet, salt and baking powder in a bowl, add 2–3 tablespoons of water and mix into a dough. Gently roll out the dough on a floured surface until it is around 1cm/½in thick. Roughly trim to dimensions fractionally smaller than the perimeter of the casserole dish and lay the suet pastry over the stew, which, depending on the meat being used, should have been simmering for 30–40 minutes. Cover the dish and simmer for a further half an hour. Brown the crust by placing the dish under the grill for 5 minutes prior to serving.

A full suet or pastry crust can be added to any game or, as in this instance, individual-sized portions make an interesting alternative.

Puff Pastry

The common problems associated with making puff pastry are those of the pastry becoming hard and tough – normally caused by adding too much water and not enough fat to the flour. If the pastry refuses to rise, the fat may have been too warm – make sure the dough is rested well in-between rolling. Avoid pastry becoming soggy in the middle – this is due to undercooking. Makes 450g/1lb:

225g/8oz plain flour
225g/8oz cold butter
½ teaspoon of salt

Sift the flour and salt into a large mixing bowl and take 30g/1oz of the cold butter, cut into cubes, then rub into the flour. Then mix in enough cold water for the mix to form large, rough clumps of dough. Turn the mixture onto a lightly floured surface and quickly but gently knead into a ball. Wrap in cling film and refrigerate for a minimum of 30 minutes. Flatten the remaining 200g/7oz of butter into a 2cm/1in-thick rectangle.

Roll out the dough on a floured surface into a rectangle that is three times the length of the butter and a little wider than the width of the butter. Place the butter in the centre of the dough, then fold over each dough flap so that the butter is completely covered.

Use a rolling pin to lightly press down on each edge so that the butter is sealed in. Turn the dough 90-degrees clockwise. Roll out the dough so that it returns to its previous length (three times that of the butter). Then fold over the two ends as you did when covering the butter, press the edges with the rolling pin and turn 90-degrees clockwise once more. After resting the pastry, replace on the floured surface in the position that you left off and continue with a further two rolls and 90-degree turns. Refrigerate for at least another 30 minutes and then continue with two more rolls and 90-degree turns. Wrap and refrigerate until needed.

Game Suet Pudding

Use any suitable selection of game removed from the bone and prepared in the way as described below for pies. Add some chopped winter vegetable to the stock for a little extra taste, if you like. As this is a pudding rather than just a topping, you will need more suet crust than you would for making the previous recipe. The following quantities should suffice:

450g/1lb flour
225g/8oz suet
½ teaspoon baking powder
Pinch of salt

Add cold water to the flour and suet, mixing together well until you have a dough. Split the mixture into one-third and two-thirds, shaping the latter portion into a ball before rolling it out on a floured work surface until it is around 1cm/½in thick. Use this to line a 1.4ltr/2½pt greased pudding basin. Add the game filling and a few tablespoons of thick stock. Roll out the remaining third of suet pastry until it is roughly the correct dimensions for a lid. Moisten the edges of the lining and attach the lid, trimming the surplus away with a knife. Crimp the lid and lining pastry together by pressing between thumb and forefinger. Place a cover of greaseproof paper over the top, remembering to leave a little space for the suet pastry to expand: tie it tightly around the rim of the pudding bowl with butcher's string. To make it easier to lift the bowl in and out of the cooking pan, you can either make a strong, folded strip of kitchen foil and pass it under the bowl and back up each side in order to form a sort of handle, or use the traditional method of wrapping the bowl in a muslin parcel tied at the top.

Place the bowl in a pan and add kettle-boiled water until it comes about a third of the way up the outside of the bowl. Simmer with the pan lid laid loosely in position for a couple of hours, checking occasionally to see that the pan is not boiling dry – if it looks likely, top up to the original level with more boiling water.

PIES

It seems that in years gone by, many regions had their own pie particular to the locality. Of course the most famous of these must be the Leicestershire Melton Mowbray pork pie, but others included: the 'squab' pies of Devon – not, as one might suppose, made of young pigeon, but of mutton and apple; the Shropshire pie containing rabbit meat; and the Coventry pie, which unlike its Devon counterpart, did actually consist of pigeons.

Almost any meat can be included in a game pie, but the most commonly used is that of pheasant, partridge, pigeon, wild duck, venison, rabbit and hare. It is a good way of using older birds, leaving young ones for roasting and stir-frying.

To prepare the meat it can be cubed and marinated prior to being browned off in oil in a heavy-bottomed frying pan, or even simply cut and browned in order to seal the meat. Alternatively, place bird carcasses in a large pan together with seasoning and a bouquet garni before covering with stock or water and simmering with the lid on until the meat begins to part from the bone and can be cut away in good-sized pieces. After taking off the best pieces; break up the remains of the carcass and return to the pot. Continue simmering to create a thick stock for later use (*see* Chapter 15). If the pie you are making is intended to be eaten cold, one way of ensuring that the filling sets after cooking is to include a pig's trotter in with the stock ingredients.

Mini Game Pie Surprises

Served cold at picnics, the 'surprise' comes from the fact that a quail egg is included in each of these delightfully tasting pies. The quantities below make 12 pies:

350g/12oz mixed game meat, cooked and finely chopped
12 quail's eggs, soft-boiled and shelled
1 small bunch each of spring onions, chives and parsley; all of which should be finely chopped
1 egg
pinch each of salt, black pepper and chilli flakes
350g/12oz shortcrust pastry

Leave the eggs to one side and mix together the meat, herbs and seasoning. Roll the pastry on a floured surface and, with a 9cm/4in pastry cutter, prepare 12 discs and line 12 muffin tins. Bake blind in a pre-heated oven gas mark 6, 200°C/400°F for 5–10 minutes or until the pastry is dry and just beginning to colour. Brush the pie interiors with beaten egg whilst still warm and half-fill each with game meat before adding a quail egg in each and topping off with more meat filling.

Cut out another 12 shortcrust pastry discs with a 7cm (3in) cutter and moisten the edges of the partially cooked cases with egg before placing the lids and pressing them gently into place. Use the remainder of the egg to glaze the lids. Bake for about 15 minutes before reducing the oven temperature to gas mark 3, 160°C/325°F and cooking for a further 20–25 minutes or until the tops look golden and firm. Remove from the oven and leave the pies to stand as they are for 5 minutes, before cooling properly with the aid of a wire rack.

Raised Game Pie

Serves 4–6
680g/1½lb game meat
225g/8oz sausage meat
300g/11oz hot-water crust pastry
115g/4oz streaky bacon
115g/4oz mushrooms
2 teaspoons each of freshly chopped marjoram, sage and thyme leaves
1 egg
300ml/10fl oz aspic or gelatine
salt and pepper

Preheat the oven to gas mark 6, 200°C/400°F, and roll out two-thirds of the hot-water crust pastry on a floured surface and use it to line a greased pie mould. Place a layer of bacon at the base of the mould then cover with a layer of half the sausage meat, then a layer of game, the remaining sausage meat and finally the mushrooms, seasoning well with the herbs, salt and pepper between each layer.

On a lightly floured surface, roll out the remaining pastry so that it is just large enough to make a lid and cover the pie. Press the edges together to seal and trim off any excess pastry, reserving the trimmings for decorations. Decorate with the pastry trimmings, brush with beaten egg to glaze and cut a hole of about 12mm/½in diameter in the centre to allow steam to escape. Bake for 30 minutes, then reduce the heat to gas mark 2, 150°C/300°F and bake for a further 1½ hours. Remove the pie from the oven and allow to cool. Heat the aspic in a saucepan over a low heat until just melted, then pour into the cooled pie through the steam vent using a funnel. Chill for 6–8 hours before serving.

NB Try marinating the game meat with the herbs and some port for 4–8 hours before starting the recipe.

Perfect Pigeon Pie

Serves 4
6 pigeon breasts
3 rashers bacon, chopped
1 onion, finely chopped
115g/4oz mushrooms, chopped
2 hard-boiled eggs, sliced
280ml/½pt game stock
seasoning
170g/6oz flaky pastry

Cut the pigeon breasts into cubes and flour lightly. Place in a deep pie dish, together with the onion, mushrooms, egg and bacon, and season well. Add the stock. Roll the flaky pastry into a lid and lay over the dish, remembering to cut two vents. Cook at gas mark 9, 240°C/475°F for 15–20 minutes. Remove and cover the pastry lid with cooking parchment before returning to the oven and cooking for a further hour at gas mark 5, 190°C/375°F.

Venison Sausage Pie

With the vast array of sausage meat available, any would make a good basis for this quick and easy pie. Venison does, however, work very well.

Serves 4
225g/8oz sausage meat
225g/8oz short pastry
1 medium onion
1 teaspoon mixed herbs
2 eggs, beaten

Line a pie plate with half the pastry. Mix together the sausage meat, chopped onion, herbs, 1 beaten egg and place the mixture on the pastry. Cover with remaining pastry, taking care to seal the edges well by brushing a little of the second beaten egg yolk around the sides. Make a small vent hole in the centre in order that the steam might be allowed to escape, and brush more egg mixture over the pastry top. Bake at gas mark 7, 220°C/425°F for 30 minutes. Cool completely before packing for a picnic.

Rook Pie

The Kings Arms, Didmarton, Gloucestershire have an annual Rook Supper. Although there is a long tradition of eating rook pie throughout the country, this particular venue apparently came about as the result of a ready supply of rook meat provided by the gamekeepers of the nearby Badminton Estate, and is as good a place as any to go and taste rook pie if you don't fancy the idea of doing it yourself.

Originally, 12 May was the official rook-shooting day in most parts of the countryside and was chosen because it was the time when the majority of young rooks were leaving the nest. Known as 'branchers', they were easy to shoot with specially made rook rifles and the young meat was very tender, making a pie a popular meal, especially for the poor and latterly during World War II, when meat was very scarce.

Along with grey squirrel meat (*see* Chapter 13), rook pie looks set to become once again a popular 'alternative' dish for those who wish to try something a little different, but, as only the breast and top part of the thighs of rooks are edible, and the back and skin meat is bitter and black, the birds must be skinned and carefully sorted before cooking. There are, of course, many variations on a theme and rook meat prepared as above can be substituted in any recipe given for wood pigeon.

Serves 4
8 rook breasts
8 pheasant/partridge/chicken livers (optional)
225g/8oz diced lean ham
225g/8oz flaky pastry
12 small white onions, peeled
170ml/6fl oz Burgundy wine
170ml/6 fl oz game or chicken stock
2 carrots, finely chopped
85g/3oz butter
seasoning
1 egg

Melt the butter in a frying pan, then flour, season, and brown the rook breasts on both sides for about 10 minutes without letting them burn. Add the white onions, ham and wine before cooking for a further 5 minutes.

Transfer all into a large, buttered baking dish; add the chopped carrot, the stock and the livers (if you have them). Cover with pastry, cut vent-holes and brush with beaten egg yolk. Bake the pie in a hot oven gas mark 7, 220°C/425°F for 10 minutes and then reduce the oven temperature to gas mark 4, 180°C/350°F and bake for a further 30–35 minutes or until the crust is golden. Serve hot from the baking dish.

Rabbit Pie

In *The Game Cook* (Crowood, 1988), author and cook Carolyn Little suggests that a simple rabbit pie can be made in the following way:

Serves 4
1 rabbit, jointed
280ml/½pt stout
115g/4oz ham, chopped
1 onion, chopped
1 carrot, chopped
1 parsnip, chopped
55g/2oz turnip, diced
seasoning
225g/8oz puff pastry
milk

Season the rabbit joints with salt and pepper. Pour the stout over and leave to marinade for 8 hours. Afterwards, place the rabbit and stout in a pan and add the ham and vegetables. Cover and simmer over a low heat for 1½–2 hours, or until tender. Add a little stock if necessary. Pre-heat oven to gas mark 5, 190°C/375°F.

Remove the rabbit from the pan and allow to cool slightly before separating the meat from the bones. Chop the meat and place in a pie dish. Spoon the stout and vegetables over and mix with the rabbit. Roll out the pastry and place over the pie dish. Glaze with milk and cook in the oven for 25–35 minutes or until the pastry is well risen.

Carolyn suggests serving with baked potatoes and runner beans.

Pheasant Weaves

Vary the taste by including several types of game bird meat.

Serves 4
225g/8oz pre-cooked pheasant (thighs from a roast and/or breast meat)
85g/3oz mushrooms, sliced
1 small onion, finely chopped
425ml/¾pt milk
55g/2oz butter
55g/2oz flour
1 egg, beaten
seasoning
225g/8oz puff pastry

Roll out the pastry to a shape measuring roughly 30cm/12 in × 26cm/10in.

In a pan, melt the butter and sauté the mushrooms and onion, taking care not to let the butter burn. Spoon in the flour and add the milk, stirring constantly until the mixture begins to thicken. Add the pheasant and set aside to cool. Place the pastry on a greased baking tray and spoon the mix lengthways down the centre of the puff pastry, folding the shorter edges over the filling. Down each of the long sides, make eight cuts towards the centre and weave them alternatively over the pheasant filling. Brush with the beaten egg before cooking in an oven at gas mark 5, 190°C/375°F for 30–40 minutes or until golden brown. Serve with Jersey potatoes and salad.

Rabbit and Macaroni Pie

For this recipe, the rabbit has been pre-cooked and the meat removed from the bones.

Serves 4
meat of 1 rabbit
55g/2oz boiled macaroni
55g/2oz grated Cheddar cheese
425ml/¾pt milk, warmed and thickened with cornflour
egg, beaten
seasoning
450g/1lb rough puff pastry

Roll out and use two-thirds of the pastry to line a pie dish. Bake blind, using the methods outlined at the beginning of this chapter. Fill by laying macaroni, rabbit and cheese until the ingredients have all been used. Pour in the thickened milk, roll out a lid from the remainder of the pastry and seal the edges well by brushing with a little beaten egg. Slit to vent holes and brush the lid with the rest of the beaten egg. Bake in a hot oven for 1 hour.

Rabbit and Venison Sausage Crumble

Although not technically a pie, due to having no pastry topping or casing, this is a variation on the rabbit pie recipe.

Serves 4
1 rabbit, jointed
340g/12oz venison sausage meat
225g/8oz onions, chopped
115g/4oz fresh breadcrumbs
1 tablespoon fresh herbs, chopped
game stock
30g/1oz butter
seasoning

Place half the sausage meat in a casserole and lay the rabbit joints on top. Sprinkle with the chopped onion and herbs. Place the remaining sausage meat on top. Half-fill the dish with stock before covering with breadcrumbs, pressing down well and placing small knobs of butter on the top. Cover with foil, and cook in an oven at gas mark 2, 150°C/300°F for 1½ hours or until the rabbit is tender. Remove the foil 15 minutes before the end of the given cooking time in order to allow the topping to brown.

Simple Fish Pie

Similar to the above, this recipe also uses a crumble-type topping. Any flaky substantial fish can be used, but salmon and/or trout seem to work well.

Serves 4
340g/12oz cooked fish, flaked
3 hard-boiled eggs, shelled and chopped
4 medium tomatoes, skinned and sliced
2 tablespoons spring onions or chives, very finely chopped
425ml/¾pt cream or white sauce (*see* Chapter 15)
115g/4oz grated Cheddar cheese
115g/4oz fresh breadcrumbs

Arrange the fish, eggs and tomatoes in layers in a greased ovenproof dish, stir the chives or onions into the sauce and pour over the layers. Mix together the cheese and the breadcrumbs and spread over the top of the mixture. Bake at gas mark 4, 180°C/350°F for 15 minutes or until the top is crisp and golden.

Fish Quiche and Fish Loaves

Because of its moist nature, it is very difficult to make true fish pies with pastry. With a little imagination and experimentation, it is, however, possible to try several variations on a theme. Try precooked or smoked salmon or trout flaked into a quiche (*see* Quiches and Tarts, page 123), or covering the ingredients of a basic fish casserole with a rich puff or flaky pastry crust.

Also try using small cottage loaves or similar sized rolls to form a casing for any fish pie filling. Remove the top from the loaves or rolls and carefully scoop out all the inside, leaving just the crusty walls. Brush them inside and out with melted butter, place on a baking sheet and bake at gas mark 7, 220°C/425°F for 5–10 minutes. Fill with a warmed fish filling: using the previously removed bread 'tops' as a lid if so wished. Serve with green salad.

Bread loaf with a warmed salmon, cucumber and cheese filling.

Salmon Loaf

Serves 4
450g/1lb fresh salmon, skinned, boned and chopped
115g/4oz frozen prawns
700ml/1¼pt milk
140ml/½pt whipping cream
55g/2oz Cheddar cheese, grated
55g/2oz butter
3 eggs
5 tablespoons plain flour
2 tablespoons freshly chopped parsley leaves
1 clove garlic, crushed
2 teaspoons anchovy essence
seasoning

Lightly grease and base line a 1.4ltr/2½pt loaf tin or straight-sided ovenproof dish. In a saucepan, melt half the butter. Add the garlic and stir in 3 tablespoons of flour; cook for a couple of minutes, until a roux is formed. Remove from the heat and gradually stir in 425ml/¾pt of milk. Bring to the boil, simmer and stir until it thickens and is without lumps.

In a blender, purée the sauce, salmon, cream, eggs, seasoning and anchovy essence. Spoon half the mixture into the loaf tin or dish, sprinkle with parsley and half the prawns before adding the remainder of the fish mixture. Cover tightly with buttered baking parchment. Place in a roasting tin and add boiling water until it comes about halfway up the sides. Cook in the oven at gas mark 2, 150°C/300°F for about 1¾ hours.

About 10 minutes before the end of cooking time, make a sauce to accompany the dish by heating the remaining milk, butter and flour in a pan. Stir continuously and once the sauce has thickened, add the cheese and the rest of the prawns. Remove the paper from the loaf and place a serving plate over. Invert, lift off the cooking container, spoon a little sauce over the loaf, serving the rest separately in a sauceboat or gravy jug.

Trout, Salmon and Coarse Fish

In her honour, we had eels with dill sauce, followed by wine jelly. She
seemed to consider this an everyday country meal, for she munched the eel
with about as much pleasure as if it had been mince.

(Ilse, Countess von Bredow, Eels with Dill Sauce – Memories
of an Eccentric Childhood; English translation, 1990)

Karl Marx often told enquirers that his favourite food was fish and his preferred drink, brandy. Not
a bad combination I must admit but, generally, a crisp white wine is a better option for most kinds of
fish. Try Muscadet, Sancerre and Pouilly Fumé; young Chablis, dry Champagne or Vinho Verde.

TROUT

The most easily available trout is undoubtedly rainbow, no matter whether it be bought from the
supermarket or given to you by a friend who enjoys fishing at one of the many trout fisheries
throughout the country. Some can be amazingly good, especially when taken from chalk streams or
a fishery privileged enough to be served by clear unsullied waters. Others, unfortunately, can taste
very muddy and unpleasant when cooked – much depends on their origins and on what they have
been feeding.

Nothing, however, can beat the freshly caught and gutted wild brown trout simply pan-fried in
butter or wrapped in tinfoil and cooked either in the oven or over the hot coals of a barbecue.
Before enclosing in tinfoil, liberally smear the fish with butter and add a squeeze of lime juice. Wild
brown trout rarely get too big, but, irrespective of whether it is brown or rainbow being cooked,
allow roughly 10 minutes per 450g/1lb at gas mark 4, 180°C/350°F.

Shop-bought trout are easy enough to come by.

Easy, Herby Trout

Easy enough to cook at the best of times, this recipe is made even quicker by the use of a microwave. In fact, it could just as easily be included in Chapter 11.

Serves 4
1 × 900g/2lb trout (or approximate weight)
115g/4oz wholemeal breadcrumbs
rind and juice of small lemon
30g/1oz chopped almonds
4 dessertspoons chopped fresh dill (or fennel)
2 dessertspoons olive oil

Open and gut the trout. Mix together all the ingredients to create a stuffing and place in the cavity of the fish before putting it into a microwave-proof dish. Cover with a few small knobs of butter, sprinkle with black pepper and baste with honey before baking on a high heat for 5 minutes. Serve with lightly steamed green vegetables and small new potatoes.

Trout Pasta Pots

Serves 4 (as a starter)
225g/8oz cooked and flaked trout removed from the bone
225g/8oz small spiral pasta
1 small carrot
1 spring onion, finely chopped
½ red capsicum, finely chopped
2 tablespoons chopped parsley
3 tablespoons mayonnaise
4 tablespoons single cream

Boil the spiral pasta for 10 minutes or as per the manufacturer's instructions. Put the trout flakes into a bowl and mash it gently with a fork. Grate the carrot into the trout. Add the spring onion, mayonnaise, cream, capsicum, parsley and pasta to the bowl and mix the ingredients together well before spooning the mixture into four small ovenproof pots (ramekin dishes are perfect). Bake for 15 minutes at gas mark 4, 180°C/350°F or until heated through. Serve straight away.

Trout in Oatmeal

Serves 4
4 trout fillets
3 eggs
1 cup milk
¾ cup flour
1½ cups oatmeal
seasoning

Mix and whisk together the eggs and milk. In a bowl (or a large strong polythene bag), mix the oatmeal, flour and seasoning. Dip each trout fillet in the milk/egg mix and then coat them well with the oatmeal mix, leaving them to stand for 5 minutes before frying in hot oil, 'round' side up. Add more oil if the original gets too hot or smoky. Leave the fillets 'fat' side down all through cooking. Lift carefully from the pan when done and lay on a sheet or two of kitchen roll until the excess oil has been absorbed. Serve with the usual fish garnishing of tartar sauce and lemon wedges.

Smoked Trout Soufflé

I must admit that, passable though my other cooking skills are, I've never yet managed to master the art of a soufflé – the last time I tried making small ones as a starter, I was left with ramekin dishes containing not very much at all, whilst the oven was filled with soufflé mixture! I am, however, assured that this particular recipe works well!

Serves 4

85g/3oz cooked smoked trout, flaked
200ml/7fl oz fresh milk
30g/1oz butter
4 separated eggs
1 extra egg white
a few onion and carrot slices
6 peppercorns
1 bay leaf
2 tablespoons plain flour
seasoning

Place the milk, onion and carrot slices, bay leaf and peppercorns into a saucepan and bring to the boil. Remove from the heat, cover and leave for 30 minutes before straining and keeping the milk. Put the milk, flour and butter back into the cleaned saucepan and heat slowly, stirring all the time. Once the sauce has thickened, simmer for 1–2 minutes, remove from the heat and add seasoning. Let the mixture cool before adding the 4 egg yolks, one at a time, and beating them into the mixture. Next, stir in the flaked trout.

After whisking all the egg whites until they are of a meringue consistency, mix 1 tablespoon of egg white into the sauce mixture before, very gently, pouring and folding the sauce into the bowl of egg whites. Pour the soufflé mixture into a greased 1.4ltr/2½pt soufflé dish and carefully level off the top (at this stage, the mixture should only fill three-quarters of the dish but, judging from my own experience, what it does in the oven is anybody's guess!). Place on a baking tray and cook at gas mark 4, 180°C/350°F for about half an hour, at the end of which time it should be well-risen, golden brown on top, firm to the touch yet slightly soft in the centre.

Smoked Salmon and Trout Terrine

The usual flavours of trout and salmon are subtly altered in this terrine by the addition of smoked haddock and mackerel.

Serves 4–6 as a starter; more when used as a sandwich filling
450g/1lb smoked haddock
115g/4oz smoked mackerel fillets, skinned and halved lengthways
225g/8oz smoked trout fillets, skinned
115g/4oz smoked salmon fillets, skinned and halved lengthways
½ cucumber, halved lengthways with the seeds removed and finely diced
½ onion, peeled and sliced
1 bay leaf
115ml/4fl oz double cream
70ml/2½fl oz lemon juice
6 peppercorns
1 teaspoon paprika
½ teaspoon cayenne pepper
3 tablespoons fresh dill, chopped
sachet powdered gelatine
seasoning

Place the haddock, onion, bay leaf and peppercorns into a shallow pan, adding sufficient water just to cover. Bring to the boil, simmer and cook for 15 minutes. Remove the fish. Strain and reserve 115ml/4fl oz of the liquor. Flake the fish and leave to cool. Place the haddock, cream, 2 tablespoons dill, paprika, cayenne pepper and 2 tablespoons of the lemon juice into a food processor and blend until smooth. Season.

Place the reserved fish liquor into a small pan and sprinkle in the contents of the gelatine sachet. Leave to soak for 5 minutes, before dissolving over a very low heat and finally stirring into the fish mixture.

Lightly grease a 850ml/1½pt terrine, straight-sided dish or loaf tin and line with cling film. Line the base and sides with the smoked trout slices (remembering to reserve a little for the top of the terrine). Spoon a third of the blended fish mixture into the bottom of the terrine and spread evenly with the back of the spoon. Lay half the salmon and mackerel fillets on top before spooning in half of the remaining fish mixture. Add the remaining fillets as before and finish with the last of the fish mixture. Cover with the rest of the trout slices and place in the fridge for at least 3 hours. Make a cucumber relish by whisking together the remaining lemon juice and 3 tablespoons light olive oil. Stir in the cucumber and the remaining dill and season to taste. To serve the terrine, turn out onto a flat plate and remove the cling film. Cut into slices and serve with salad as a starter. Alternatively, use it as a sandwich filling for a picnic. Use brown bread spread with unsalted butter, to which a few drops of lemon juice has been added.

A simple salmon terrine looks appetizing and is the perfect starter or lunchtime snack.

SALMON

Salmon is such a wonderful fish that its delicate flavour is, to my mind, spoilt by any attempt at adventurous sauces. Can there be anything better than a salmon steak oven-baked in a parcel of tinfoil containing butter and lemon juice and served with new potatoes; or anything more subtle than a terrine?

Simple Salmon and Samphire

This is so quick and simple that it should perhaps be in Chapter 11.

Serves 4
4 salmon steaks (each about 115g/4oz)
225g/8oz samphire
olive oil
30g/1oz butter
1 tablespoon castor sugar
salt and freshly ground black pepper

Heat the grill to high and bring a large saucepan of water to the boil. Brush the salmon steaks with olive oil before placing them under the grill. Grill both sides. Whilst they are cooking, place the samphire into the boiling water, together with a tablespoon of castor sugar. Boil for only a couple of minutes, drain and incorporate the butter. Shake the pan well so that all the samphire is coated with melted butter before making a 'nest' of samphire on each dining plate and topping with a salmon steak. Serve with new potatoes and a smile!

Salmon Steaks and Fennel

Place 4 salmon steaks in an ovenproof dish. Take 2 peeled and finely chopped shallots, 1 finely chopped bulb of fennel, a bay leaf, 2 stalks of fresh chopped parsley and sprinkle over the fish. Add 140ml/¼pt dry white wine, cover tightly with foil and bake at gas mark 4, 180°C/350°F for 15 minutes. Strain off 115ml/4fl oz cooking liquor, re-use the foil to cover the fish and keep warm.

Boil the fish liquor and reduce until there is only about 1 tablespoon left. In a heat-resistant bowl, beat 2 egg yolks together and stir in the liquor, at the same time working in 55g/2oz of softened butter. Place the bowl over a pan of boiling water (as one would for melting chocolate) and whisk until all the butter has melted. Add a further 55g/2oz of butter and whisk in a similar fashion until a thick, fluffy sauce has been created. Remove from the heat and spoon a little over each salmon steak as it is plated up.

Carpaccio of Salmon

Lovely as a starter or a lunchtime meal with salad.

Serves 4
1 fresh fillet of salmon, boned
2 tablespoons olive oil
1 lime
dill
1 tablespoon pink peppercorns (substitute mixed peppercorns if not available)

Slice fish very thinly, with a sharp knife and arrange on a large plate before sprinkling with olive oil and lime juice. Season, then sprinkle with dill. Leave to chill for 10 minutes before serving.

Spinach and Salmon Lasagne

Serves 4
400g/14oz lasagne
200g/7oz salmon
1 onion
650–700g (approximately 1½lb) frozen spinach
55g/2oz butter
4 tablespoons olive oil
1 cup white sauce (*see* Chapter 15)
mixed herbs, salt and pepper

Peel and chop the onion and sauté in butter and olive oil in a heavy-bottomed frying pan for 5 minutes over a medium heat. Add the salmon and cook for a further 5 minutes. Leave to cool whilst cooking the pasta in boiling salt water as per the packet instructions. Defrost the spinach over a low heat, stirring constantly and season.

Take an oven dish and layer ingredients as follows: lasagne, spinach, salmon, onions, white sauce, until all ingredients used. Cook in an oven preheated to gas mark 4, 350°F/180°C for 30 minutes.

Sprinkle with mixed herbs and serve with salad or vegetables.

COARSE FISH

Technically, a book purporting to *Cook Game* should not include the likes of carp, eels, perch and pike among its pages, but there are coarse fishermen who would occasionally like to try what they catch and, provided that no legalities are broken by taking fish away from the water, there is no reason not to experiment. It is, after all, only in the UK where there is a reluctance to eat these types of fish – elsewhere in Europe they form a part of many an everyday meal. In fact, generations ago, carp, for example, were bred by monks in specially constructed ponds in order that they could have fish on Friday.

Pike Steaks Loire-Style

Because pike flesh can be very dry, steaks should be marinated for a time before cooking. Coat them with olive oil and crushed black peppercorns and leave them in a cool place for a couple of hours before cooking.

Serves 4
4 pike steaks (each weighing approximately 225g/8oz)
5 tablespoons olive oil
450g/1lb onions, finely chopped
2 cloves garlic, finely chopped
750g/10oz plum tomatoes, roughly chopped (you can use tinned, but remove a little of the liquid)
4 sprigs thyme
2 bay leaves
parsley, to garnish
seasoning

Fry the onions softly and slowly in 3 tablespoons of olive oil until they begin to caramelize. Add a little seasoning before transferring them to a fairly shallow ovenproof dish, which should be large enough eventually to hold the pike steaks. Spread the tomatoes over the onions and top off with the garlic, thyme and bay leaves. Use the remaining 2 tablespoons of oil to dribble over the mixture before baking, uncovered, in an oven set at gas mark 2, 150°C/300°F for 15–20 minutes.

In a hot skillet, sear the pike steaks on both sides and position them on top of the roasted tomatoes and onions. Bake for a further 10 minutes and sprinkle a little freshly chopped parsley and a few drops of olive oil over the top just before serving.

Choose a dry white Anjou or other Loire wine to drink with it, in order to add to the authenticity!

Baked Zander Pie

Zander can be cooked in the same way as cod. It may be fried in breadcrumbs or batter, grilled or baked, and also makes an excellent fish pie.

Serves 4

Bake four zander fillets in a little milk together with chopped mushrooms, herbs and seasoning for about half an hour. Drain the juice and save for making a sauce. Leaving the fish in the dish in which it has been cooked, break it into flakes with the edge of a fork. In a saucepan, melt some butter and add a little flour to make a roux: gradually mix in the juice kept back after cooking the fish and heat until the sauce begins to thicken, stirring continuously. Add a little grated cheese to the sauce before pouring it back over the fish. Top off with mashed potato and grill until brown.

Zander with White Butter

At home here in the Loire Valley, not far south of Saumur, possibly the best-known fish dish is *Sandre au Beurre Blanc*. Zander, a member of the perch family, is caught by means of traps set in the river and almost every restaurant has its own version on the menu. Basically, the fish fillets are either grilled or baked and served with a sauce made up of white wine vinegar, butter (lots of it!) and softened shallots, but I would not presume to include a recipe, for fear of being accused of 'teaching Grandmother to suck eggs'. Far better to ask for it in a restaurant when next in the region, in order to be sure of tasting the real thing.

Less well-known in the region, but none the less popular with our French neighbours, are pike steaks.

Carp Stuffed with Caviar and Capers

The principles of this recipe can be adapted to suit most coarse fish – the fish should not, however, exceed about 3kg/6½lb in weight. Carp can be quite muddy tasting, hence the reason the monks kept them in specially constructed ponds through which they could ensure a regular supply of clean water. In his book *The River Cottage Cookbook* (HarperCollins, 2001), Hugh Fearnley-Whittingstall suggests several ways of overcoming the problem (and also goes into great detail regarding the necessary removal of the pitchfork-shaped bones located between the scales of pike).

Gut and descale before thoroughly washing the carp. Pack the internal cavity with a mixture of caviar (use the cheaper 'faux' or lumpfish caviar, as it would cost a fortune to stuff a big fish with good quality Russian caviar in this way!), butter, capers and lemon juice.

Wrap in foil with a good 'glug' of white wine, sliced onions and a couple of bay leaves. Bake in an oven set to gas mark 5, 190°C/375°F for 30–45 minutes, depending on the size of the fish. Serve skinless, with a spoonful of the stuffing, accompanied by new potatoes and a green vegetable or salad.

Baked Perch in White Wine

Despite being members of the same family, perch have many more bones than zander. Be aware of the fact, but don't let it put you off trying this recipe.

Serves 4
4 medium-sized perch
55g/2oz butter
dry white wine
fish stock
chopped parsley
seasoning

With a knife, score each side of the fish in two or three places. Rub the fish with salt and pepper and place them in a well-buttered baking dish, adding equal parts of white wine and fish stock until they are almost covered. Smear the butter in rough knobs over each of the perch and cover with a buttered paper. Bake in an oven gas mark 6, 200°C/400°F for around 20 minutes, basting the fish frequently with cooking juices or even melted butter. Remove the paper and return the dish to the oven for a few minutes. Afterwards, arrange the fish on a serving dish and keep warm without allowing them to dry out.

Pour the liquid from the baking dish into a saucepan and heat until it has reduced. Add finely chopped parsley before pouring the sauce back over the fish. Garnish with triangles of fried bread, lemon quarters and sprigs of parsley.

Larded Pike

Generally, smaller pike are best baked whole, in the same way that one would with trout, either coated in olive oil or butter, inside and out, or stuffed with a mixture of breadcrumbs, bacon, leafy herbs and onion. As a variation on this theme, try Larded Pike.

Serves 4
1 pike (approximately 2kg/4½lb)
24 anchovy fillets
2 teaspoons each of grated onion and grated shallots
2 teaspoons each of parsley, chives and chervil
1 clove garlic, crushed
2 large mushrooms, very finely chopped
butter for greasing paper and ovenproof dish
pinch each of cayenne pepper, sea-salt and ground peppercorns

Along the ridge of the pike, draw the point of a sharp knife just deep enough to cut the skin. Remove the skin on both sides of the fish and 'lard' with anchovy fillets (about 12 on each side). Trim them off evenly in line with the shape of the pike. Butter a piece of baking parchment cut large enough to envelope the fish and spread it thinly with a mixture of onion, shallots, mushrooms, garlic, parsley, chives and chervil. Season with cayenne, salt and ground peppercorns.

Wrap the larded pike in the paper and fold the edges of the paper together as tightly as possible. Place the whole thing in a buttered ovenproof dish (traditionally, this would have been earthenware) and pour around it approximately 140ml/¼pt dry white wine. Bake covered in an oven at gas mark 4, 180°C/350°F for 40–45 minutes. Before serving, unwrap the fish and place it on a heated plate. Scrape the herb mixture from the paper and add to a jug of mustard sauce.

To make the sauce:

280ml/½pt fish stock (*see* Chapter 15)
2 tablespoons white wine vinegar
2 teaspoons prepared mustard
2 tablespoons flour
1 level teaspoon sugar
2 egg yolks

In the top of a bain marie or double boiler, blend together the mustard, flour, sugar and a pinch of salt. Stir in the fish stock and wine vinegar, stirring constantly until the mixture is smooth and begins to thicken. Remove from the heat; add 2 egg yolks, slightly beaten, and cook, again stirring constantly from the bottom of the pan until the sauce thickens some more. (This sauce can be served hot or cold, but always with fish.)

Boiled Pike with Oysters

Purely out of interest, and not actually expecting anyone to attempt it, I enclose the following, taken directly from a very old book written many years ago by a lady called Hannah Wooley. The spelling is as printed.

Take a fair Pike and gut it and wash it, and truss it with the tail in the mouth, then take white Wine, Water and Salt with a bundle of sweet herbs, and whole Spice, a little Horse-radish; when it boils, tie up your Pike in a Cloth, and put it in, and let it boil until it swims, for then it is enough. Take the Rivet [?!] of the Pike, and a Pint of great Oysters with their Liquor, and some Vinegar, large Mace, gross Pepper, then lay your Pike in a Dish with Sippets [a type of crouton], and then heat these just named things with some Butter and Anchovies, and pour over it; garnish your Dish as you please.
(From *The Queene Like Closet or Rich Cabinet…*;
original publication date unknown)

Eels Marinara

Serves 4
1.5kg/3½lb eels, skinned
140ml/¼pt olive oil
4 cloves garlic
2 small onions, finely chopped.
4 tablespoons concentrated tomato purée diluted in a cup of water
200ml/7fl oz dry white wine
zest of ½ lemon
pinch of dried mixed herbs
seasoning

Sauté the onions, garlic, grated zest of lemon and dried herbs in the olive oil (use a large saucepan). When the garlic cloves show as being golden brown in colour, remove and discard. To the pan add the eels, chopped into 5cm/2in pieces and cook for 5 minutes, turning the eels periodically. Add the diluted tomato purée and the white wine. Cook slowly for 10 minutes; season and simmer for a further 5–10 minutes, or until it is very thick.

Buttered Eels

Quick and simple!
Serves 2
680g/1½lb fresh eels, skinned
225g/8oz unsalted butter
juice of a lime
sea salt
black pepper
chopped parsley for garnish

Chop the eel into 5cm/2in pieces and place in an ovenproof dish before adding butter, diced into knobs. Season with salt and pepper, and the lime juice. Cover the dish with damp baking parchment and a lid and cook on a low heat until the eel flesh feels soft at the point of a knife. Sprinkle with chopped parsley and serve with steamed carrots and mashed or boiled potatoes.

Eels marinara.

Fast Food – Feed the Kids

The bird was brown and burnt in one place, so they determined to eat it and not spoil it by over-roasting.

(Richard Jefferies, *Bevis, the Story of a Boy*, 1882)

The term 'fast food' is nowadays synonymous with certain American eating-place franchises and is often looked on as being derogatory – this is certainly not the case in game cookery when the freshest and purest ingredients are being used. Fast food can provide a tasty lunchtime snack or a television supper, and is a great way to introduce young children to the delights of game at a time in their life when they might turn up their noses at the prospect of a rich casserole or unusual dish. It would, for example, be surprisingly easy to encourage youngsters to eat Ostrich Burgers (*see* below) together with a plate of Game Chips (*see* Chapter 14), but perhaps not such a simple task to persuade them of the delights of Ostrich Steaks with Nutmeg Creamed Spinach (*see* Chapter 13).

Food for children should be simple – the majority are not keen on highly seasoned food. Scale down the portions so that they do not feel over-faced by what's on their plate and, with very small kids, ensure that all the portions are the same so as to avoid the otherwise inevitable cries of, 'It's not fair; they've got more (or less) than me!' Remember that in cooking for children, you are forming the basis of a lifetime's eating habits – an onerous responsibility that is undoubtedly made easier by the inclusion of some of these recipes in their diet.

FISH

There are nowadays so many opportunities to purchase farmed trout and salmon so cheaply, that not only is it easy enough to obtain, its availability and relatively low cost makes it worthwhile getting experimental and creating a few of your own 'fast food – feed the kids' recipes. There are, of course, several purists who would argue against buying farmed fish of any description, but that particular discussion has no place here. The fact remains that fish, no matter from where it is sourced, is a healthy food for children and adults alike.

Smoked Salmon Fishcakes

To make these fishcakes all that is required is a small packet of fresh smoked salmon (or trout) slices from the supermarket (off-cuts are better and even cheaper, if you can get them), a finely chopped onion, mashed potato and a little olive oil.

Whilst the potatoes are cooking, gently cook the onion in a large frying pan containing a splash of olive oil until it is soft and golden in colour. Mash the potato using a little milk and a knob of butter. Mix in the onion and leave to cool. Chop the salmon slices, either with a knife or by cutting with kitchen scissors before incorporating into the potato/onion mix.

Once the mix is just cool enough to handle with bare hands, lightly flour a chopping board or work surface and also coat your hands with a dusting of flour. Scoop out a portion of potato/onion/salmon and work into a rounded fishcake shape on the floured board. Set to one side and work on the next, whilst at the same time adding a splash more oil to the frying pan and bringing it back up to heat. Gently fry the fishcakes, turning occasionally until both sides are dark golden brown in colour. The actual length of time will obviously depend on the thickness of the cakes.

For a little extra taste, add very finely chopped chives at the time the salmon is added to the potato and onion.

Trout Marsala

Use one small trout per person and cut three slits in each side of each fish. Combine juice of a lemon, 4 tablespoons of olive oil, 1 crushed clove of garlic, 2 finely chopped green chilli peppers, a small piece of grated ginger, together with a pinch each of cloves, cinnamon, salt and pepper, and 2 teaspoons of turmeric. Spread over the fish and inside the cuts. Place sprigs of fresh coriander inside the fish. Brush the grill rack with oil or use a wire fish rack. Cook under the grill or over a barbecue for 10–15 minutes, turning often and basting with any remaining mixture.

Trout and Bacon Parcels

Take one cleaned and gutted trout per person, season inside the cavity and wrap each with two rashers of bacon. Arrange them in an ovenproof dish in such a way that the spirals of bacon cannot unwind during cooking. Bake at gas mark 6, 200°C/400°F for 15 minutes.

GAME AND VENISON

Although much has been made in the relevant chapters regarding the general need to cook game meat slowly – in some cases, after a particular joint has been marinated for several hours – in actual fact, game can, with a little knowledge and forethought, be cooked quickly under a hot heat. This makes chops of venison and strips of pheasant or pigeon breast suitable for barbecuing, grilling or stir-frying – all methods guaranteed to provide a relatively fast meal by a simple type of cooking that children immediately recognize and will not be phased by.

Pigeon Fajitas

Try using goose or pigeon breast meat to make fajitas.

Stir-fry thin strips of meat. Add chopped onions, peppers, mushrooms, mange-tout or sugar snap peas, baby sweetcorn and asparagus. Moisten with chopped tinned tomatoes or salsa.

This makes for a quick and friendly meal, where the cooked ingredients are simply placed in a single bowl at the centre of the table and everyone fills their own warmed fajitas. Serve with a green salad and, if as a quick supper with good friends, lots of wine!

Pigeon and Cranberry Crostini

Serves 4 as a light snack or finger-held 'starter'

Thickly slice a French stick or baguette, cutting at an angle to give the greater amount of surface area – depending on the length of bread, aim to get 8 pieces.

Pan-fry 8 pigeon breasts and put to one side to keep warm.

In a pan, boil the contents of 450g/1lb bag of frozen cranberries, 280ml/½pt orange juice and a little Demerara sugar until the mixture has reduced to a compote. Remove from the heat and add 50ml/2fl oz gin.

Fry the slices of French stick in hot olive oil until they are golden in colour. Remove to a serving plate. Top each piece with a spoonful of cranberry mixture, add a pigeon breast and garnish with watercress.

Crispy Pheasant Rolls

Similar to Pheasant Wrap (*see* page 162), ring the changes by using filo pastry and add to the flavour with mango chutney.

Serves 4
4 small pheasant breast fillets, skinned
8 sheets filo pastry
2 spring onions, finely chopped
55g/2oz melted butter
½ cup mango chutney
1 tablespoon sour cream

Pre-heat the oven to gas mark 4, 180°C/350°F and lightly grease an oven tray. Place the chutney, cream and spring onions into a bowl and mix well. Lay out one sheet of filo pastry and put another sheet on top. Fold in half long-ways. Place a pheasant fillet at one end and coat with a quarter of the chutney mixture. Roll the pastry once over the pheasant, fold the sides over and keep rolling in order to make a secure parcel. Do the same with the other breast fillets. Arrange all on the greased oven tray and brush with melted butter. Bake in the oven for 20 minutes or until golden in colour. Serve hot.

Pheasant Tetrazzini

Any type of game bird or wildfowl breast can be used in this recipe, but for some reason, pheasant works particularly well.

Serves 4
400g/14oz cooked pheasant breasts, cut into strips
4 rashers streaky bacon, cut into long thin strips
225g/8oz spaghetti
1 large onion, sliced
115g/4oz small mushrooms, quartered
1 green pepper and 1 red pepper, seeded, cut into strips and blanched
280ml/½pt game stock
30g/1oz plain flour
1 tablespoon olive oil
1 teaspoon concentrated tomato purée
Parmesan cheese

Cook the spaghetti in a large pan of boiling salted water as per the manufacturer's instructions. At the same time, heat the oil and gently fry the onion and bacon until the onion is soft. Add the flour and cook for 2 minutes before adding the stock and tomato purée. Stir constantly and bring the liquid to the boil. Add the peppers, mushrooms and pheasant strips. Season to taste, bring back to the boil, cover and gently simmer for 10 minutes.

Drain the spaghetti and arrange around the edge of a warmed flat serving dish. Spoon the pheasant mix into the 'well' created at the centre of the spaghetti and sprinkle with Parmesan. Serve with a salad and warm crusty garlic bread.

Pheasant Wrap

Once these pancake wraps have cooled, they could be eaten by kids as 'finger food', served with salad for lunch or as a main meal accompanied by mashed potatoes and spinach.

Serves 6
2 pheasant breasts, uncooked and very thinly sliced in the manner of smoked salmon
1 large onion, sliced and diced
breadcrumbs for coating

For the pancake wrap:

140g/5oz plain flour
1 egg
140ml/¼pt water
140ml/¼pt milk
30g/1oz melted butter
seasoning

Make the pancake wraps by sieving flour and seasoning into a bowl. Make a well in the centre of the flour; add the egg and mix together before incorporating the water and milk, beating steadily as you do so. When the mixture is smooth, add the melted butter and leave to stand for an hour.

Make 6 medium-thick pancakes in the normal way, cooking until just browned. Once cooked, stack them separated by squares of greaseproof paper until required.

Cook the onion gently in butter or oil until soft. Prepare the pancake wraps by covering each with a layer of pheasant breast and a little onion, making sure that there is a clear 'rim' left around the edge of each pancake. Brush this rim with batter and fold the edges firmly together so as to prevent the contents escaping during cooking. Brush each side with more batter and sprinkle with breadcrumbs.

Cook further by frying in oil for 5–8 minutes, turning each pheasant wrap three times.

Venison and Onion Marmalade Steaks

Use a venison fillet steak per person and pan-fry them in a little oil in a frying pan for 2–5 minutes each side, depending on how you normally like your steaks cooked. Remove from the heat; spread each steak with a little ready-made onion marmalade and top with small knobs of Gorgonzola cheese. Cook under a hot grill until the cheese has melted. Serve with new potatoes and a handful of rocket.

Deerstalker's Pie

Any leftover cooked venison makes an excellent shepherd's pie, well seasoned with tomato purée, garlic and Worcester sauce. Add variety by including sliced, steamed leeks in white sauce on top of the minced cooked venison. Alternate the topping from the usual one of mashed potato by creating a savoury crumble topping of butter rubbed into flour, on the top of which could be sprinkled porridge oats – thus keeping up the Scottish deerstalker theme.

Venison Sausage and Apple Kebabs

Cut sausage into 2.5cm/1in-thick slices. Take 4 small apples and peel and quarter them before brushing with lemon juice. Thread onto skewers, alternating with sausage pieces and 8 bay leaves. Brush with a little mild mustard and grill for 10 minutes, turning frequently.

Drambuie-Soaked Venison Kebabs

Not necessarily one for the kids, but fast food all the same!

Serves 4
450oz/1lb meat from the haunch, cut into kebab-sized cubes

Make a marinade consisting of 1 finely chopped shallot, seasoning, 1 teaspoon of cornflour, 1 teaspoon of dark soy sauce, 6 tablespoons of oil and 3 tablespoons of Drambuie liqueur. Mix well before brushing onto the venison cubes (ideally, leave them in the marinade for several hours, turning occasionally). Spike the meat onto skewers and barbecue, grill or fry, tuning frequently until the meat is crispy brown on the outside but still pink in the middle.

Doh! Ducknuts!

Someone, I'm ashamed to say that I forget whom (I don't even recognize the handwriting!), gave me this recipe 10–15 years ago. They called the recipe 'Ducknuts' so, in their honour and with apologies for failing to remember their name (and also to Homer Simpson whose catch-phrase I've borrowed!), I've given it the title I have.

Serves 4
4 duck breasts
4 fist-sized lumps of bread dough
4 tablespoons marmalade
oil

Make dough by boiling 1 medium-sized potato until cooked and save 140ml/¼pt of the cooking water. When the water has cooled to blood temperature, add a teaspoon of sugar and a teaspoon of dried yeast. Mash the potato with milk, butter, salt and 3 teaspoons sugar. Push through a sieve and add to a large mixing bowl with the yeast mix. Sieve in the flour and mix with a wooden spoon until the dough begins to form a ball. Place on a floured surface and knead the dough until it is 'springy and satiny' to the touch. Let it rise in an oiled plastic bag until it has doubled in size and then cut it into 4 fist-sized pieces.

Flatten and roll out each lump of dough until they are large enough to each wrap completely around a duck breast, with enough spare to seal the edges. Wrap a duck breast and a tablespoon of marmalade in the dough and seal firmly. Trim off any excess. Heat a few inches of oil in a wok and fry the ducknuts, turning three times in 8 minutes. Serve with mashed potatoes to soak up the juices.

Duck Quenelles with Noodles

Serves 4
70g/2½oz butter
200g/7oz cooked duck meat, chopped
115g/4oz cooked ham, finely chopped
70g/2½oz soft breadcrumbs
1½ tablespoons grated onion
1 teaspoon each of finely chopped parsley, chives and green pepper
¼ teaspoon marjoram
1 egg, lightly beaten
850ml/1½pt chicken stock
seasoning

In a pan, heat the butter and add the grated onion, finely chopped herbs and green pepper. Cook for a few minutes over a low heat, stirring almost constantly. Add the duck meat and ham, bread-crumbs, marjoram and seasoning. Remove from the heat and blend in the egg. Shape the mixture into balls roughly 2.5cm/1in in diameter and drop the balls into the boiling stock. Reduce the heat, cover and simmer for 10 minutes. Add more stock or boiling water during cooking, if necessary. Drain and serve on a bed of generously buttered egg noodles, dusted with chopped parsley and a little paprika.

Game Fondue

For the ultimate in simplicity, take the fondue set, that icon of 1970s living, from where it has been hidden in the garage all these years and use it as a way of cooking small, 2cm/1in squares of game meat. Any type will do, but for guests why not try a selection of pheasant breasts, pigeon, venison or wild boar. Spear one or two cubes of meat and hold it in the hot oil until cooked to the desired degree of 'rareness' before dipping into a sauce.

The sauces can be many and varied, but here are half a dozen suggestions that work really well: curry, sweet and sour, cheese, barbecue, garlic and fruit.

NB Children might like the novelty of 'cooking' their own meal, but there must also be adequate adult supervision; bearing in mind the fact that the fondue set contains hot oil.

SOMETHING ELSE ENTIRELY!

On the odd occasions that you happen to come across a piece of game-type meat, such as ostrich for example, there is a tendency to be a little afraid of it; either because of the expense of purchase or because it is such a rare treat that one is unsure when, or if, one will come across it again in the future. Naturally these factors make the average cook wary of experimentation and a guaranteed foolproof recipe is usually the safest option. Trimmings and off-cuts can, however, sometimes provide some 'fast food' options, such as Ostrich Burgers.

Kangaroo Pizza Wedges

Assuming that you might have a little kangaroo meat left after the recipes on pages 187–188, this might be just the thing for an unusual quick meal!

Serves 4
400g/14oz kangaroo meat, minced
55g/2oz salami, finely sliced
1 small onion, grated
1 large tomato, sliced
½ medium red capsicum, finely chopped
½ cup grated mozzarella
¼ cup dried breadcrumbs
3 tablespoons tomato purée
1 teaspoon dried oregano leaves
salt and pepper

Place the mince, capsicum, salami, breadcrumbs, oregano and onion into a large bowl. Add the tomato purée and seasoning. Knead the mixture together well. Grease a 23cm/9in pie dish and press the mixture firmly into it as if making a cheesecake base. Arrange the tomato slices over the top, sprinkle with mozzarella and bake for 20 minutes in oven gas mark 6, 200°C/400°F. Pour off any liquid, slice and serve immediately.

Ostrich Burgers with Balsamic and Tomato Relish

Without some care in preparation, ostrich cuts can sometimes be a little on the tough side, so this is a good way of utilizing some of the poorer meat on offer and also any trimmings.

Serves 4–6
500g/1lb 2oz ostrich fillet
2 finely chopped, medium-sized shallots
3 cloves crushed garlic
2 grated carrots
3 sticks peeled and chopped celery
1 small bunch parsley, chopped
2 eggs

For the Balsamic and Tomato Relish:

4 tinned plum tomatoes
6 tablespoons balsamic vinegar
4 tablespoons dark brown sugar

Trim off any fat and sinew from the meat before mincing on a medium setting (it may pay to put the meat through the mincer for a second time). Add the celery, garlic, shallots, carrot and parsley, and mix all the ingredients together. Season with salt and pepper. Beat the eggs and add to the mince and vegetables. Split and shape the mixture into 4 chunky burgers or 6 thinner ones and grill for approximately 1 minute on each side (ideally, they should be rare in the centre, but it obviously depends on personal taste) and serve on grilled buns accompanied by the balsamic and tomato relish. Make the relish by binding together the tomatoes, balsamic vinegar and sugar.

To make the most of presentation, these gourmet burgers can be served with char-grilled vegetables, such as peppers and onions.

Buffalo Steak Sandwich

Well, why not?!

1 large thick rump steak
1 sandwich loaf
115g/4oz mushrooms, chopped

Grill the steak medium-rare and fry the chopped mushrooms in butter. Cut the end off the sandwich loaf and hollow out a portion of the centre, large enough to slide in the steak and mushrooms. Put back the crust, wrap the loaf in plain, un-dyed blotting paper, then greaseproof paper, and tie into a neat parcel with string. Place under a weight for 6 hours and do not slice until required.

Special Guest Recipes

> To share knowledge and to dine with friends are the only pleasures
> nowadays left open to me.
>
> (Samuel Johnson, a diary entry made in 1782)

I cannot understand why, when so many people love game, that it is not eaten more often in homes and it remains thought of by the majority to be something that one eats in a restaurant. Fortunately, not quite everyone thinks that way and in this 'guest' section of *Cook Game*, there is a wonderfully eclectic range of dishes.

Although approached in connection with this book, Gordon Ramsay was, unfortunately, prevented by 'contractual obligations' from supplying a recipe. He does, however, feel that game is often best cooked simply, with respect and by the following of traditional methods. Game is, he says, 'Man's food – it has the whole hunter-gather feel about it.'

Faison de Chez Jacques

There is a small bistro at Loudun, in the Vienne region of France. Well known by gourmands in the area, one illustrious client of old was René Monory, who eventually became known as the 'father' of Futuroscope – the world-famous technological theme-park at Poitiers. This was his favourite and it is now the current patron's 'signature' dish.

Just how many the quantities given actually serves depends on the appetite, but Jacques feels that everyone should eat a whole pheasant! To my mind, this recipe should amply serve two people and, if the pheasant is quartered rather than halved, could easily be stretched to four.

1 pheasant
1 glass dry white wine
½ glass pastis (Ricard or Pernod)
1 small tub crème fraîche
200g/7oz button mushrooms
4 tomatoes
3 carrots
2 onions

2 cloves crushed garlic
1 bulb of fennel
olive oil
paprika, salt and pepper

Joint the pheasant into halves or quarters and brown off in a heavy-bottomed casserole dish with the aid of a little olive oil. Prepare all the vegetables and slice the carrots, fennel and onion, and cut the tomatoes into quarters. Add the vegetables, tomatoes and mushrooms together with a ladleful of cold water. Cover and simmer for 5 minutes. Add half the pastis, the white wine, crushed garlic, paprika and seasoning, and cover again before simmering for a further 30 minutes. Add the crème fraîche, stir and leave to simmer for 3 minutes.

Remove the pieces of pheasant, place the vegetables on a plate and cover with the sauce. Finally, in a small pan, heat the rest of the pastis in order to flambé the meat. Place the pheasant pieces in the centre of the vegetables and serve hot.

Faison de Chez Jacques.

Country Pheasant Casserole

Bryan Ferry, best-known as the front-man of Roxy Music, song-writer and passionate supporter of the Countryside Alliance, suggested this recipe, adapted from *The Aga Book* (Mary Berry, Aga-Rayburn, 1995), saying that he finds it 'just the sort of thing for a wintry evening in the country!'

Serves 4
2 tablespoons olive oil
30g/1oz butter
1 pheasant
115g/4oz chopped streaky bacon
45g/1½oz flour
280ml/½pt red wine
300ml/½pt game stock
2 tablespoons bramble jelly
1 tablespoon Worcester sauce
1 teaspoon thyme
salt and pepper
16 button onions
a little gravy

Heat the oil and butter in a large casserole dish, add the pheasant and fry quickly to brown. Lift out onto a plate and leave on one side. Fry the bacon in the pan for about 3 minutes and then lift out with a slotted spoon and add to the pheasant. Stir the flour into the fat remaining in the pan and cook for a minute. Gradually blend in the wine and stock, bring to the boil, stirring until thickened. Add the remaining ingredients, return the pheasant to the pan with the bacon, cover with a lid and bring back to the boil. Simmer for 5 minutes before transferring the dish to the floor of the oven for about 3–4 hours, until the pheasant is tender. Lift the pheasant out of the pan, take the meat off the bone and return the meat to the sauce. Taste and check seasoning. Reheat and serve with creamy mashed potato and a crisp green vegetable.

Pigeons with Cherries in Eau-de-Vie

Not all French film actresses are opposed to field sports! As well as being an actress, Émilie Courtat is a well-known breeder of German pointers, which her husband Thierry Lacour, a photographer, uses when flying his birds of prey. 'My husband occasionally brings home a couple of pigeons as a result of his hobby. *Pigeon aux cerises et à l'eau-de-vie* is a quick, simple and very tasty recipe!'

Serves 4
4 pigeons
85g/3oz butter
680g/1½lb firm cherries, washed and de-stoned
eau-de-vie (or cherry brandy)
salt
pepper, freshly ground

After plucking and dressing the birds, remove the heads, feet and wing tips. Keep back around 20 of the cherries for the final presentation. Salt and pepper the pigeons; put 55g/2oz of the butter into a *cocotte* (casserole dish) and brown the birds thoroughly on all sides. Add a tablespoon or two of eau-de-vie (or cherry brandy) and the main bulk of the cherries. Cover the dish and leave to simmer for about 15 minutes, turning the pigeons' mid-way through. Take the birds from the casserole, cut each into two and keep somewhere warm.

On the heat, deglaze the dish with another tablespoon of eau-de-vie and the remainder of the butter. Adjust the seasoning by adding a little more freshly milled pepper. Add the cherries previously held back, cover the sauce and the cherries, and leave for 5 minutes more. Place the half-pigeons onto a serving plate and spoon over the cherries and amalgamated cooking juices before finally decorating with five cherries still with the stalks attached. Apparently, a bottle of Beaujolais Crus, such as St Amour, goes exceptionally well with this particular French dish.

Venison Casserole in Beer

This is one of Jane Robins' personal favourites – she and Alan know it as 'Bambi Stew'! (*See* also Goose and/or Pigeon Stir-Fry, page 175.)

Flash-fry cubed venison in order to seal all sides before placing the meat in a casserole dish along with whole button mushrooms and whole baby onions. Add the contents of a can of beer (John Smith's or similar), cover and cook at gas mark 3, 160°C/325°F for approximately 40 minutes before thickening the liquid with gravy granules or a 'thickening' of your own choice. Lower the oven heat to gas mark ¼, 110°C/225°F and continue cooking the casserole for a further 4 hours, stirring occasionally.

Hand-Raised Grouse and Foie Gras Pie with Apricot and Wild Mushrooms

Martyn Nail, the Executive Chef of Claridge's Hotel, Mayfair, kindly agreed to share this recipe saying:

> The hand-raised pie is a British classic, which done well is still very much enjoyed today. It is a feature on the winter menus when the game items are in season. Guests like to come down to the kitchen and see it prepared, as it always draws interest. This wonderfully crafted pie is so scarcely seen and understood these days.

Serves 8–10

To make the hot-water pastry:

300ml/10fl oz milk
300ml/10fl oz water
350g/12oz lard
1.350kg/3lb plain flour
2 teaspoons salt
egg wash – 2 egg yolks to equal amount of cold water

For the filling:

5 grouse, bones removed and flesh checked for shot
1 'lobe' of duck foie gras
200g/7oz mixed wild mushrooms
15 dried apricots
8 leafs gelatine
30ml/1fl oz ruby port
15ml/1 tablespoon Madeira
10g/¼oz salt
white pepper
2 sprigs of thyme

For lining the pie:

500g/1lb 2oz streaky bacon
Consommé jelly:
500 ml chicken consommé
10 leaves gelatine

Heat the water, milk and lard to 85°C. Put the flour and the salt on to a bench and form a 'well' in the centre. Gradually add the liquid to the flour, stirring as you do so. Work the ingredients lightly to form the pastry. Wrap in cling film and chill. Allow the pastry to come to room temperature then roll out to 0.4cm/¼in. Cut the pastry to the shape that best fits and line your chosen mould (remembering to reserve some pastry in order to form the pie lid).

Line the greased mould with pastry, making sure to overlap the edges and press it tightly into the tin, leaving a 3cm/1¼in border of pastry protruding over the edge of the tin. Line the pastry with streaky bacon.

Place all the ingredients for the filling in a bowl and mix in the seasoning. Allow to stand for 1 hour before arranging the filling in the pie, forming a mosaic pattern. Close over the bacon and bring up the over-lapping pastry. Now prepare your lid and make one or two steam holes, brush the pastry with an egg wash and decorate. Brush the top of the overlap with the egg wash and apply the lid to the pie. Allow to rest for at least half an hour before cooking.

Cook at gas mark 6, 200°C/400°F until golden (approximately 15 minutes), then cover with foil and cook until you get a core temperature of 54°C. Allow to rest at room temperature for 25–30 minutes and then cool in a fridge for 1 hour until the pastry sets.

Soften the gelatine in cold water and bring the consommé to the boil. Add the gelatine and allow to cool. Then pour the prepared jelly through the steam hole: allow this to set in the fridge for 20 minutes before toping up with the jelly again. Repeat this process until the jelly reaches the top of the steam hole.

Allow to stand for at least 24 hours before removing the pie from the mould and slicing.

Jugged Hare in Chocolate

The country writer and journalist, Duff Hart-Davis, admits to not being able to 'cook for toffee', but he is, however, 'a great fan of jugged hare, particularly when it's done with chocolate'. The following might just fit the bill.

Serves 4–6
1 hare, skinned and jointed
12 shallots, peeled and chopped
12 button mushrooms, halved
55g/2oz plain flour
3 tablespoons olive oil
½ (75cl) bottle of good red wine
1 teaspoon red wine vinegar
1.1ltr/2pt game stock
bouquet garni
30g/1oz paprika
15g/½oz fresh oregano, finely chopped
55g/2oz raisins, soaked for some time in 115ml/4fl oz brandy
1 cup of strong expresso coffee
4 squares of bitter dark chocolate

Coat the hare joints in flour and paprika before browning in the oil placed in a heavy-bottomed casserole dish. Remove and put to one side. Brown the shallots in the same oil before removing them also and de-glazing the dish with the vinegar. Return the hare and onions to the casserole dish and add wine, stock, mushrooms and the bouquet garni. Bring the liquid to the boil, skim off any unpleasant-looking fats and simmer very gently for 45 minutes. Add the brandied raisins, coffee and chocolate and stir until the sauce is thickened (you may need to increase the heat for this). Serve from the dish after finally sprinkling the jugged hare with the chopped oregano.

Goose and/or Pigeon Stir-Fry

Jane Robins' partner Alan is an enthusiastic wildfowler and she tells me that they 'never buy meat from the butchers, as there's always so much in the freezer. This means I have to be imaginative when it comes to thinking of different things to do with wildfowl.' She's the creator of the *Stuffed Goose Breast* recipe (*see* page 63) and also suggests that minced geese and pigeon breasts make a good alternative to minced beef when it comes to cooking chilli dishes or making burgers.

For a simple stir-fry, cut goose and/or pigeon breasts into thin strips. Place a little oil in a wok or large frying pan and cook the meat for a minute (turning frequently) before adding any combination of finely sliced ginger, spring onions, peppers and any other stir-fry choice of vegetables. The important thing with a stir-fry is, as the name suggests, to stir constantly as the food cooks and not leave it on the heat until it loses its crispness.

To achieve a colourful and tasty stir-fry it is, as the name suggests, important to cook fast, turn constantly and use a fairly high heat.

Salmon Stuffed with Crab and Spinach with Dill Sauce

'This is such an easy recipe and looks fantastic on the plate, so if you want to impress your friends give this a try', says Chris Tarrant, television personality and keen fisherman.

Serves 4
4 salmon fillets
100g/3½oz fresh crabmeat
200g/7oz fresh spinach, sautéed and finely chopped
1 clove garlic, finely chopped
½ bunch fresh dill
½ltr/1pt full fat milk
1 level teaspoon soy sauce

Take the salmon and with a sharp knife cut a small pocket into the middle of the salmon. Mix together the crab, spinach and garlic and stuff into the salmon

Cut a large piece of tinfoil and place the salmon on top, leaving 1cm/½in between each fillet. Add the milk, soy and dill to salmon and close to form a parcel. Cook at gas mark 4, 180°C/350° for 10–12 minutes.

Serve hot with a little of the sauce on top of the salmon (be careful not to overcook the salmon – it should be pink on the inside).

Pheasant – Baden-Style

Ernst, the Count von Baden, still lives in his home country of Germany, but he shoots, fishes and periodically stalks roe deer in the UK. 'Despite having a plentiful supply of game in the woods at home, Britain has the best shooting and stalking of anywhere in the world. This is a simple and favourite recipe from home.'

1 pheasant
1½ teaspoons salt
¼ cup melted butter or margarine
1 tablespoon brandy
1 teaspoon grated lemon rind
¼ teaspoon powdered thyme
1½ cups water
1 tablespoon flour

Sprinkle ½ teaspoon salt over inside of bird. Place bird on a rack in a shallow roasting pan. Combine the butter/margarine, brandy, lemon rind, ½ teaspoon salt and thyme, and brush the bird generously. Roast in a moderately hot oven for 50–55 minutes, basting often with the butter mixture. Combine giblets, water and remaining salt in a saucepan and cook until tender. Remove giblets. Strain the broth and save. Remove the bird and skim off fat. Stir flour into 1 cup of the broth; return to pan. Cook over low heat, stirring constantly until thickened, and pour over pheasant.

Like the recipe for Faison de Chez Jacques (*see* page 168), this should amply serve two and, if the bird is quartered could, at a pinch, be stretched to four.

The Count also suggested the accompaniments of Bavarian Bread Dumplings (*Bayerische Semmelknödel*) and a Vegetable Medley (*Leipziger Allerlei*).

For the Bread Dumplings:

Peel, boil and mash potatoes until very smooth. Beat in an egg and ¾–1 cup of flour, adding just enough to make an easily handled dough. Form several 5cm/2in balls. Fry 1 slice of bread, cut into cubes and press a cube of bread into the centre of each potato ball. Bring a large pan of water to the boil and, once boiling, drop in the dumplings. Simmer for 20 minutes. The dumplings are done when floating and slightly puffed up.

For the Vegetable Medley:

Heat 1 cup of beef stock in a large saucepan and add about 140g/4oz each of small cauliflower florets, peas, asparagus spears (cut in half), sliced mushrooms and 200g/7oz baby carrots. Simmer for 8–10 minutes. Add 4 tablespoons of flour and 2 teaspoons of salt to ¼ cup of cold water and blend until smooth. Pour and stir into the vegetables. Cook over a low heat, stirring constantly until the sauce has thickened. Spoon into a serving dish and garnish with 2 hard-boiled eggs, peeled and quartered.

Salmagundi

Sarah Kennedy, proprietor of The Sun Inn at Helpin, West Yorkshire, is responsible for an annual summer get-together, traditionally held after a fun clay shoot organized by the local shooting syndicate. It has now become a tradition that they supply her with various game birds from their freezers, with which she creates her version of Salmagundi – a well-known northern salad-type dish. Sarah says:

> It's difficult to get the balance right so that the trenchermen in the party think they've had a good meal, but the lighter eaters don't go away feeling stuffed! Also, in late June, when the clay shoot is held, you don't want the same heavy food as you would after shooting on a cold winter's day – this seems to keep everyone happy. Normally, I do this recipe for 16–20 people so I've roughly halved the quantities.

With regard to the grouse, Sarah says, 'Based where we are, usually someone has a couple knocking about somewhere, otherwise use another type of bird comparable in size or add an extra bird each to the two previous'. And as for the peas, 'One of the shoot members is a keen gardener so vegetables are always his contribution to the meal. If you're not so lucky, use frozen peas.'

Serves 8
2 mallard
2 pheasants
2 grouse, if available
450g/1lb peeled potatoes
450g/1lb carrots, cut julienne-style
450g/1lb peas
225g/8oz tomatoes, sliced
1 cucumber, sliced
4 sticks celery, sliced
4 hard-boiled eggs, shelled and halved
140ml/¼pt oil
70ml/2fl oz lemon juice
pinch each of sugar and mustard powder
seasoning

Season and place the grouse and pheasants on their backs in a roasting tray. Place the mallard breast-sides down on a rack set above the tray. Roast at gas mark 6, 200°C/400°F for roughly 1 hour or until the birds are obviously cooked (cooking time will be longer than when roasting a single bird). Allow to cool until it is possible to insert a knife along the breast bones and remove the breast meat from the bone. Cut into thin strips, each about 5cm/2in long.

Boil the potatoes, drain and allow to cool before finely dicing. Boil the carrots until *al dente*; drain and rinse in cold water. Boil the peas, making sure they are still firm; drain and cool. Using a large serving dish, first of all place all of the diced potato and some peas at the bottom. Follow by arranging some of the strips of carrot and some slices of cucumber, alternating each with strips of assorted types of game meat. Pour over a little dressing made by whisking together the oil, lemon juice, sugar and mustard powder, together with a little seasoning. Add more slices of cucumber, game meat, peas and strips of carrot. Keep building up the layers, sprinkling each one with the dressing as you do so. For the penultimate layer, use the slices of tomato and top off with any remaining meat, peas, carrot pieces and celery. Arrange the halves of hard-boiled egg and garnish with a few stuffed olives if desired.

NB To make this cold-meat salad more visually appealing, make sure that, as each layer is added, each is slightly smaller than the previous one in order that a pyramid effect is created.

Salmagundi.

Gamekeeper's Tandoori

Jack Hughes is a regular writer for *Countryman's Weekly*. His features are always witty and informative and I was delighted when he sent his unique recipe for Gamekeeper's Tandoori, together with the following observations:

> As a keeper, I am often disappointed by the lack of imagination shown with game. 'We are fed up with pigeon pie or rabbit stew' is the cry, so why not do something a bit different? Pheasant, partridge, rabbit or squirrel work in most chicken recipes and venison or Canada goose can be substituted for beef. We have a great source of natural, free range food, so let's use it with a little more flair... I reckon that game works particularly well in Indian cooking and for beginners who don't know a Bhuna from a Korma, this recipe is an ideal starting point – it is not going to burn your mouth, has bags of flavour and kids usually love it too.

Serves 4

900g–1.35kg/2–3lb young rabbit legs or pheasant breasts
juice of 2 medium lemons
2 cups plain yoghurt (a good organic variety is ideal)
salt
4 tablespoons sunflower oil
1 teaspoon chilli powder
1 teaspoon black pepper
pinch ground nutmeg
¼ teaspoon garam masala powder
¼ teaspoon saffron threads, dissolved in water before using or, alternatively, use red food colouring
2.5cm (1in) piece fresh ginger, grated
4 cloves fresh garlic (less if you are a garlic-phobe!), crushed
6 green chillies

NB Chilli powder varies in strength, so be careful. In my experience, the lighter red stuff is often hotter – so it is wise to err on the conservative side!

Split the green chillies, remove seeds and chop.

NB A word of warning: the juice from fresh chillies stays on your hands, so do not inadvertently rub your eyes or scratch your nose, as you will suffer the most unpleasant stinging sensations. The best way to avoid this, it to use the thin latex gloves available at chemists.

Put the yoghurt, sunflower oil, chilli powder, black pepper, nutmeg, garam marsala, saffron or red colouring, fresh ginger, garlic and green chillies into a food processor and whisk until smooth.

Take the rabbit legs or pheasant breasts and score with a knife, in order to allow the spices to penetrate. Mix lemon juice and salt and rub over meat – this removes the 'film' that often occurs on the meat – and leave in a bowl for 1 hour. Pour the yoghurt/spice marinade over and cover well with cling film and keep in fridge for a minimum of 12 hours, but up to 3 days is even better.

Take out the rabbit or pheasant, remove excess marinade and place either on a barbecue or under a hot grill, turning frequently for around 10 minutes. Brush with a little oil or butter during cooking and hey presto – an instant Gamekeeper's Tandoori. Sprinkle with fresh coriander leaves and serve with Basmati rice, mango chutney, a vegetable curry and tuck in!

As Jack says, 'The beauty of this recipe is it is simple to make, works with any game meat, is always popular on shoot lunches and is a bit of a change from the norm.'

Young Pheasants in Parcels

Tuscan chef, restaurateur and cookery writer, Antonio Gamba, whilst declining to submit a specific recipe, nevertheless had a few thoughts regarding game cookery in his home country, and included tips likely to be of use to those wishing to *Cook Game*.

> Italian cooking is like the country itself: colourful, happy, generous, and exuberant. Game is a real Tuscan delight, pungent and never dull. From *Fagiano al Tartufo* [pheasant stuffed with truffles] to *Lepre in Agrodolce* [hare with pine kernels, sultanas and chocolate], Tuscany offers a broad range. More peasant food is the rabbit cooked with olive oil and casseroled slowly in the good company of shallots, bacon, garlic and wine for 2–3 hours. Slow cooking, yes, for the meat of all but the youngest game is fibrous and dry. Young pheasants you can simply fry in butter, season with salt and pepper, herbs and lemon peel, before baking them for a brief 10 minutes in individual pots or greaseproof bags. The older bird, be it pheasant or partridge, needs something more to soften and moisten the meat, such as wrapping it in cabbage leaves and bacon for a long, slow simmer in stock.

The Lady Friend's Pike Pie

In 1988, I had cause to meet the late Sir Michael Hordern, the great British actor (and the voice behind Paddington Bear!), in connection with a BBC radio programme I was planning. Very much a keen fisherman, he told me of a strange encounter on the riverbank:

> Many years ago while fishing at night for sea-trout on the Dart, I heard (but couldn't see) a figure on the opposite bank, also fishing, singing wordlessly, the choral Last Movement of Beethoven's 9th Symphony. When she paused I took it up and thereafter antiphonally. We met by daylight and became life-long friends.

As well as Beethoven, the mystery lady apparently also had a great fondness for Pike Pie, which she insisted on eating accompanied by champagne!

After boiling in a fish kettle, top, tail and skin the pike – taking great care to remove the rather treacherous bones situated between every flake of flesh along its back. Flake and season the meat before mixing with a tin of sweetcorn and laying it in a greased ovenproof dish, together with a little fish stock (from the kettle if you have cooked the pike yourself). Top off with mashed potato and grated cheese and cook as you would a Shepherd's Pie. Serve with braised fennel (and champagne!).

Grilled Partridge with Garlic, Oil, Lemon and Cayenne

This recipe by Clarissa Dickson-Wright is a very simple way of cooking tender young red-legs that don't have a great deal of flavour of their own, but respond very well to grilling. It makes a quick dish for hungry shots. You need to cut the partridges through the back and flatten them out. It is also a dish that can be cooked over the embers of an open fire out of doors.

4 tablespoons olive oil
4 cloves garlic, crushed
juice of 1 lemon
4 partridges, spatchcocked
1 tablespoon of cayenne
salt and pepper

Mix the oil, garlic and lemon juice together and marinate the partridges for 1–3 hours.

Take them from the marinade, season and sprinkle on the cayenne. Grill, turning from time to time for about 15–20 minutes. Be careful not to overcook, and baste them with the marinade from time to time.

Something Unusual –
Something for Free

If I were a cassowary
On the plains of Timbuctoo,
I would eat a missionary,
Cassock, band, and hymn-book too.
(Impromptu verse supposedly by Bishop Samuel Wilberforce,
but also ascribed to William Makepeace Thackery)

It is becoming increasingly possible to purchase 'exotic' meat in the UK, by which I mean ostrich steaks, imported kangaroo meat, buffalo joints, shark steaks and, on occasion, I've even seen crocodile for sale. Although none of them can be classed as game, the majority do, however, feature the same healthy-eating options as some of the more conventional game fare. The meat is lean and the texture similar to that found in venison, for example.

It had always been my intention to include at least one shark recipe in *Cook Game* but, unlike kangaroo meat, for example, where meat is derived from a sustainable source, it appears that the decline of some shark species is as a direct result of their demand as an unusual restaurant dish. It is estimated that annually, more than 3,300 tonnes of shark meat and fins are consumed in Britain alone, putting increasing pressure on the 28 species of shark, including blue, spurdog, basking, thresher, porbeagle, tope and dogfish (rock salmon), which inhabit UK waters. One of our greatest beliefs as countrymen is that all game stocks should be sustainable. For this reason alone, I have refrained from including any shark recipes in this book.

There are others that can in no way be described as exotic: rooks and grey squirrels are an everyday sight, no matter whether you live in the rural wilds or only have occasional access to a city park. At first glance, they do not suggest a ready meal, but young rooks have always been a part of the countryman's seasonal diet and it was only after the Second World War that its use in rook pies (for which we have included a recipe on page 134) became less popular. The grey squirrel, long accepted as a pest and shot as such by foresters and farmers, seems to be becoming increasingly trendy as a source of potential meat – not least because of it being championed by various 'survival' programmes and 'back-to-nature' cooking chefs on prime time television. To see wild birds and animals such as these killed for food seems more acceptable now than it was 15–20 years ago when I was briefly involved in a countryside-oriented TV programme for the BBC.

Of course, it is not possible to buy rook and squirrel meat in the same way that it is ostrich and even kangaroo, but if you can make a friend of a sporting countryman, or even your local game dealer, who may well be prepared to tell you the name of the best person to contact, you may be able to get a few 'samples' for free.

Something for free is always an attractive proposition: some may be lucky enough to be given the occasional game bird or rabbit and others may pick them up easily as a result of their chosen field sport. The countryside can, however, offer much more in ways affiliated to a book on game cookery. Wild mushrooms (provided that they can be correctly identified) are so much more tasty than the bland shop-bought ones; a bramble jelly picked and made by yourself is a lot more interesting when accompanying a plate of grouse or hare than is a spoonful of a supermarket product, and wild-picked herbs thrown on the embers of a barbecue can enhance even an ordinary piece of meat with their subtle taste. Follow such a meal with a glass of homemade sloe gin and I would suggest that life couldn't get much better!

'Something Unusual – Something for Free' is, therefore, the ideal title for this particular chapter and it will, I hope, give quite literal 'food for thought'.

SOMETHING UNUSUAL

It sometimes happens that, as you wander around the tented food halls of a country fair or agricultural show, you come across a choice of meat that is a little unusual. It is also an ever-increasingly simple matter to buy 'exotic' meats online. Personally I'm like Oscar Wilde, who famously said that one should try everything once; but there is often the problem that, having bought a piece of meat because 'it would be nice to try', one is unsure just what to do with it.

Crocodile

Crocodile meat is a white meat and its nutritional composition compares favourably with that of more traditional meats. It has a delicate flavour, is low in fat and high in protein and, according to 'Kezie Foods', one of the UK's largest suppliers of exotic meats, it is best cooked frozen as, during the thawing process, all the meat juices run out and the flavour is lost. 'Kezie' advise that crocodile steak tail fillet should be cooked for 2 minutes on either side and then allowed to stand for a few minutes. It is best served just cooked (in red meat terms, medium rare). Do not use a large number of ingredients, other than herbs or spices and, if frying, always use butter or olive oil, as they will not impart a conflicting flavour to the meat.

Crocodile Tail Steak Fillet

Serves 4
4 × 170g/6oz tail steak fillets
55g/2oz butter
1 clove garlic, chopped
8 shallots, peeled and chopped
2 tablespoons redcurrant jelly
2 tablespoons dry sherry
½ cup fresh cream

Melt the butter in large heavy frying pan and gently fry the garlic and shallots until tender. Remove from pan, leaving the butter. Turn heat up to hot, and quickly sear both sides of the crocodile steaks, as described above, before setting aside the fillets to rest.

Return garlic and shallots to the hot pan along with redcurrant jelly and sherry. With the mixture simmering, add cream and stir until of even consistency, but do not allow to boil at this stage. Serve fillets with the sauce poured over.

Kangaroo

For those would-be consumers who worry about the importing of meat from an animal's native country, it is good to know that all are protected by certain government restrictions. To both protect and control kangaroo numbers, for example, the population is monitored by Australian Government conservation agencies, who issue annual quotas for harvesting as part of their Government Kangaroo Management Programme. Kangaroos are only 'harvested' from primary producing regions, with no animals being harvested from National Parks or conservation areas.

Kangaroo is a lean, succulent, versatile, red meat. It is also rich in iron and is a fine-grained meat that, when cooked, has a texture likened to liver. Having a low fat content (less than 2%) means it is very easy to over-cook, so it is best served rare or medium rare with a reddish or pinkish colour inside.

Kangaroo can be prepared in a variety of ways using wet or dry cooking methods. To help retain its moisture, it is suggested that the meat is brushed with a little olive, sesame or peanut oil prior to cooking and, if you're pan-frying the meat, to quickly seal both sides in a hot pan.

Kangaroo steaks can only be sold frozen so, as a very rough guide as to how much meat you may need, 450g/1lb will be required for 4 people. Fillet and rump steaks are all suitable for pan-frying, grilling, or barbecuing. Kangaroo sausages have a strong game flavour and a very distinctive taste: a 350g/12oz-pack serves 2–3 people. Burgers are generally sold in packs of 4, weighing approximately 115g/4oz per pack.

The following two recipes were kindly supplied by Osgrow, 7b Boyces Avenue, Clifton, Bristol, BS8 4AA, England.

Kangaroo with Kiwi, Cashew Nuts and Dates

Serves 4
450g/1lb fillet or steak
2 kiwi fruits,
12 dates, stoned
115g/4oz cashew nuts
brown game stock (*see* Chapter 15)
cream
pepper and salt

Season the kangaroo meat with salt and pepper to taste. While frying the meat, finely chop half of the nuts and ⅓ of the dates. Take the meat out of the pan and keep it warm. Put the chopped nuts and dates into the pan. They should gently brown before the brown stock is added. Allow everything to cook through and finish with a dash of cream.

Pour the sauce onto serving plates, allowing it to cover the surface before laying the steak over it and garnishing with some slices of kiwi, dates and the remaining nuts. Serve with new potatoes.

Kangaroo with Mango and Coconut

Serves 4
500g/1lb 2oz kangaroo meat
2 mangoes, peeled and cut into strips
55g/2oz grated coconut
2 tablespoons coconut milk
2 tablespoons game stock
140g/5oz butter
1 dessertspoon Demerara sugar
pinch each of cinnamon, salt and pepper

In a heavy-bottomed frying pan, gently heat roughly two-thirds of the butter and cook the mangoes. Once they are cooked *al dente*, remove from the heat but keep warm.

Season and pan-fry the meat, remove from the pan and keep warm. Add the coconut milk and stock, and season to taste before cooking further in order that the sauce created thickens and reduces. Complete the sauce by adding the remainder of the butter.

Finally caramelize the partially-cooked mango slices in some sugar. Before serving, arrange a bed of mangoes on the plates, slice the meat into thin slices and arrange like a fan over the mangoes. Spoon sauce over the kangaroo and sprinkle with grated coconut and allow to brown a little under the grill.

Ostrich

If you have never eaten ostrich before, simple pan-frying is perhaps the best way to enjoy this tender, succulent meat at its best. The low fat content naturally means that cooking should be quick and the meat should be served pink – it is far better to undercook than overcook an ostrich steak. It is possible to create a great meal using little more than olive oil, a little sea salt and freshly ground black pepper. For something easy but with a little extra added, try the following recipe.

Ostrich Steaks with Nutmeg Creamed Spinach

Serves 4
2 ostrich fillet steaks
2 portions fresh leaf spinach
grated nutmeg
4 tablespoons natural yoghurt
olive oil
seasoning

Slice the steaks to make four. Prepare spinach for cooking and steam until it wilts. Purée and add seasoning, grated nutmeg and yoghurt. Reheat but do not boil. Place olive oil into the frying pan and heat to smoking. Cook the ostrich steaks to medium rare and serve surrounded by creamed spinach, with sautéed potatoes.

Ostrich and Date Brochette in a Spicy Marinade

Serves 4
Ostrich steak, cut into 8 2cm/1in squares
8 dates, pitted and cut in half
sesame seeds

For the marinade:

1 clove finely chopped garlic
1 teaspoon fresh ginger
1 teaspoon cinnamon
1 teaspoon fresh coriander
2 tablespoons sunflower oil

Mix the marinade ingredients into a bowl and season. Add the ostrich cubes, stirring well to cover, and leave for 2 hours. Roll the dates in the sesame seeds. To cook, put two pieces of ostrich and two dates alternatively on a skewer and cook under a hot grill or over a hot barbecue for about 10 minutes, turning to ensure that all sides are cooked evenly.

Rook

Along with grey-squirrel meat, rook meat looks set to become once again a popular 'alternative' dish for those who wish to try something a little different, but, as only the breast and top part of the thighs of rooks are edible, and the back and skin meat is bitter and black, they must be skinned and carefully sorted before cooking. Basically then, use only the breasts of young birds.

Rook Lyonnaise

Serves 4
8 rook breasts
sufficient milk to cover the rook breasts when soaking
flour
1 beaten egg
115g/4oz breadcrumbs
oil
2 large onions, peeled and cut into thick rings
1 tablespoon sherry vinegar

Soak the breasts overnight in the milk. Drain and dry them, then coat in the flour, dip in the egg and then in the breadcrumbs. Heat the oil and fry the onion until crisp and brown before draining on kitchen paper. Wipe the pan with the paper and pour in more oil. When the oil is hot, fry the breasts for about 4 minutes on each side or until golden brown.

Mound the onion rings in the centre of a dish and arrange the breasts in a circle around it. Drain off the oil, swill out with a few drops of the vinegar and pour as a sauce over the rook breasts.

Squirrel

The following two recipes are, I think, American, courtesy of Dan, our 'backwoods-man' friend. He advises that the scent glands, which are found in the small of the back and under the forelegs, should be removed and that the carcasses should be washed thoroughly inside and out with hot water – 'never wash them after jointing'. It may, in fact, pay to treat squirrels in much the same way as for the majority of rabbit recipes and marinade the joints overnight in lightly salted water.

Squirrel and Dumplings

Serves 4
2 squirrels, dressed and jointed
2½ cups of water
parsley
1½ teaspoons salt
pinch black pepper

For a recipe for Dumplings, *see* Chapter 14.

Place the squirrel joints into a pan and add the water and salt. Heat until boiling and then cover the pan, reducing the heat until the water is just very gently simmering. Cook for 2–3 hours (depending on whether the squirrels are young or old) or until the meat feels tender. Add the salt, pepper and chopped parsley, and increase the heat until the liquid boils. Lay dumplings over the top of the squirrels, cover tightly and cook for 15–20 minutes.

Squirrel Fricassee

Serves 4
2 young squirrels, dressed and jointed
½ onion, grated
½ cup softened butter
½ cup flour
½–¾ cup water
1½ cups milk
seasoning

Combine the seasoning and flour and dredge the squirrel pieces in the mixture, making sure that each piece is well coated. Heat the butter in a heavy-bottomed frying pan or skillet and gently brown the pieces on all sides until they are a rich brown colour. Add ¼ cup of the water, cover tightly, reduce heat and simmer gently for approximately 30 minutes, or until the meat feels tender. Add remaining water, as required. Once the meat is cooked, remove to a hot platter and cover with foil to keep hot.

Blend the leftover flour into the juices remaining in the pan, gradually add the milk and cook until the gravy thickens, stirring constantly. Add the onion and cook for a minute or two more before pouring over the squirrel pieces and serving immediately.

Snails

I'm sorry, but I just had to include this!

The English garden snail (*Helix aspersa*) has a unique subtle flavour and was, at one time, regularly eaten in parts of the West Country. The traditional method of dealing with them is to starve them for a few days, soak them in water for a further 24 hours and then cook for 3 minutes in rapidly boiling water before rinsing them off.

The cleaned snails, still in their shells, are then simmered in a stock made up of cider, water (⅓ cider to ⅔ water, in case you are interested!), chopped onions, herbs and seasoning, for 3–4 hours until they are ready to be prised from their shells. Mixing together butter, grated cheese and cream, to which is then added a combination of finely chopped herbs and seasoning, makes a herb butter that is spooned into each shell. The snail is then replaced before being grilled for perhaps 30–60 seconds. Lovely!

A country hedgerow can often provide a wide variety of natural and organic ingredients.

SOMETHING FOR FREE

We all like to think that we're getting something for nothing, but there is also a sentiment that if we've not paid for it, it cannot be much good. Never has this been less true than when considering the natural crops and harvests of the countryside where, with a little knowledge, we can pick accompaniments and ingredients for the various recipes in this book, which are often better quality and certainly fresher than those that we pay for. In some instances, it's also possible to enjoy new taste sensations that would be impossible to buy commercially – I cannot, for example, ever see the day when some of our major stores will stock nettles or dandelion leaves: on the other hand, if they discover that there is money to be made from doing so, who can tell?

Try and select harvesting sites that are not regularly sprayed and avoid picking the likes of brambles from busy roadside hedges, where they may be affected by exhaust fumes. Depending on what it is you are after, in the majority of cases (nettles may, however, be excused from this one), one should always leave enough of anything to ensure that it can regenerate. Check too that you are not breaking the law by picking certain species of vegetation and fruit.

Mushrooms

Mushrooms are the natural partners of game and, as the famous chef and fungi aficionado, Antonio Carluccio, points out in his book, *A Passion for Mushrooms* (Pavilion Books, 1989), in parts of Italy, where both are found in excess, it is not unusual to find restaurants where the menu is made up entirely of these two ingredients.

Some types of fungi will only grow in certain types of soil: morels, for example (and there is a recipe for Guinea-Fowl with Morels on page 82), prefer the edges of broad-leaved woodland, whereas the easily recognizable field mushrooms are found in open fields and meadows – doing so, they confound the theory that mushrooms only grow well in damp, shady places.

The different types of fungi come into season at different times of the year, but it is a traditional autumn treat to be out and about in the early morning. Only look in places where chemical fertilizers and sprays have not been used, as most types of mushroom spores will not tolerate such treatment. Carry a basket rather than a plastic bag in order to prevent damage to the mushrooms and, most importantly, *make sure that you know without doubt exactly what you are picking*. A good field-guide containing excellent photographs, rather than line illustrations, is essential.

Herbs, Weeds and Seaweed

As a source of wild herbs, the countryside cannot be bettered. If you know what you are looking for and the time of year you are most likely to find a particular herb, it should be possible to pick wild garlic, chives, fennel, horseradish and chervil (cow parsley) in most parts of the British Isles. The cultivated varieties of these have been included time and time again throughout the numerous recipes in this book and there is no reason whatsoever why they should not be substituted by their wild relations. Some are definitely seasonal – the wild garlic, for example, seen growing in many places, but particularly on the roadside banks of Cornwall, is only available during April/May time, whereas wild chives can be found almost all the year round. We are lucky here in France where, in some parts, it's possible to find wild asparagus, the young shoots of which are often cooked in omelettes.

Make some useful, interesting and unusual cooking oils by adding a sprig or two of wild herbs into a bottle of good quality olive oil and letting it infuse or make various flavoured vinegars by the following method.

Put 1.1ltr/2pt white wine vinegar into a pan and heat to just below boiling point, then leave to cool. Wash and dry the bottles you intend to fill with vinegar and place about 4 sprigs of herbs in each one. Pour in the cooled vinegar and seal the bottles. Stand on a sunny windowsill for a couple of weeks and then put in a darker place for long-term storage.

The rabbit recipe on page 99 shows that young nettles make an excellent substitute for spinach and can be used as an accompaniment to many game and fish dishes. Steam and serve fat-hen, good-king-Henry and chickweed in exactly the same way.

Chickweed and dandelion leaves can be used in the Classic Green Salad (see page 210), but beware of using too much of the latter – not for nothing is it known as 'piss-the-bed' by many countrymen, due entirely to its diuretic properties. Only pick young leaves and soak them for a time in water before including in a salad.

Pickled Samphire

We have used samphire in two of the recipes in this book; it can be bought, but it is obviously better if you can pick your own for nothing! It grows on estuaries below the high-tide mark and can be eaten raw, as described elsewhere in this book, or boiled and served with butter in the same way as asparagus. It also makes a great pickle that can be served with all manner of fish and game dishes. Fill a Kilner jar with samphire, add some peppercorns and a little grated horseradish. Pour over a boiling mixture of dry cider and vinegar mixed in equal quantities and leave for a few weeks.

Laver Bread

Make traditional laver bread to eat with stews or with a fried breakfast of venison liver, kidney and a slice or two of wild boar pancetta from the laver seaweed. Soak it for a few hours in fresh water in order to rid it of the saltwater in which it has been growing. Dry it in the bottom oven of the Aga or outside in the sunshine (assuming that there is some!) and blend it down in a food processor until it becomes powder. Boil the powder for some time (traditionalists suggest 4 hours), drain it and dry it, and it's ready for that breakfast fry-up.

Dulse Chips

Dulse is a reddish type of seaweed that grows along the northern coasts of the Atlantic and in Northern Ireland is a well-known snack food. From June to September it is picked by hand at low tide and left out in the sun to dry before being either eaten as it is, or ground to flakes or powder to be used in the same way as above. It can also be pan-fried into chips, baked in the oven covered with cheese or even eaten straight from the sea.

Nuts and Berries

A chestnut stuffing goes well with pheasants and we have included recipes in the relevant chapter in which it's possible to use either bought or, preferably, home-picked fresh chestnuts. They do require skinning before use, but that is not too difficult if you follow the method given on page 16. Use as large chestnuts as you can find and use them quickly, for they soon dry out and/or go mouldy.

Hazelnuts are common enough to find in the summer, as they are forming, but not so easy when they are ripe in the autumn, due to the fact that squirrels and small mammals have generally got there before you! Walnuts are found in some places and both can be shelled and toasted in a shallow baking tin at gas mark 2, 150°C/300°F before being added to dishes in much the same way as described in the recipe for Curly Kale with Wild Boar Pancetta and Pecan Nuts, page 117.

Pears Filled with Hazelnut and Cheese-balls

Try serving a half pear stuffed with hazelnuts and cheese as an interesting side garnish for game.

55g/2oz hazelnuts, crushed or minced
115g/4oz cream cheese
4 pears, peeled, cored and halved

Toast the hazelnuts until lightly browned. After preparing the pears, scoop a hollow out of each half in order to accommodate a cheese-ball. Dip each in lemon juice to prevent them from turning brown. Add a pinch of salt to the cream cheese and make into small rounds, which should then be rolled in the toasted, crushed hazelnuts. Fill the hollows in each pear half and serve alongside almost any game bird (with the exception of grouse or pigeon).

Blackberry Dressing

The possible uses for blackberries in game cooking are infinitesimal: make jellies, chutneys, add to sauces, or fill a Kilner jar with fruit, top it up with white wine vinegar and leave in a sunny, warm position for a couple of weeks. Strain out the fruit so that you are left with pure liquid before bottling and storing in a cool place. Use as a dressing over game meat salads.

Jellies and Chutneys
Jellies and chutneys make a fine accompaniment to game dishes and several have been mentioned as being particularly good with certain types of meat such as grouse, hare and venison. Redcurrant is a particular favourite, but to make that you will have to grow your own or raid someone's garden! Try 'wild' alternatives by experimenting with cranberries, juniper berries, bilberries and, if you can find them, cranberries (found wild in certain areas). Crab apples and orchard fruits also make a good basis for jellies and chutneys that can be served with many dishes.

Pear and Mint Jelly

5 large sprigs fresh mint
115g/4oz finely chopped mint
2.2kg/5lb pears, peeled and chopped
280ml/½pt cider vinegar
1.1ltr/2pt water
granulated sugar

Put the pears into a pan with the sprigs of mint and add the water. Bring to the boil and then simmer for about 30 minutes or until the fruit is soft and pulpy, stirring occasionally. Add the vinegar and boil for a further 5 minutes. Strain the contents of the pan overnight and the next day, measure the strained juices. For every 570ml/1pt of liquid you have, add 400g/14oz sugar. Put the mixture into a preserving pan and boil rapidly for about 10 minutes until setting point has been reached (105°C/221°F). To test, spoon a little of the jelly onto a chilled saucer, allow to cool and then gently push your finger across the surface – it should 'wrinkle' if ready. Allow the mixture to partially cool and add the chopped mint. Pour into clean dry jars, seal and store.

Crab Apple Chutney

2.25kg/5lb crab apples, peeled and cored
225g/8oz dates, stoned
115g/4oz raisins and/or sultanas
225g/8oz onions, minced
6 chillies
450g/1lb Demerara sugar
570ml/1pt vinegar
1 tablespoon salt
1 tablespoon powdered ginger

Place all the ingredients, together with a little of the vinegar into a pan, bring to the boil, and add more vinegar as required until all is absorbed. Stir well until the fruit is soft and the mixture is of a thick consistency. Place in clean warm jars, cool, seal and store.

Elderberries
Elderberries can be used in a number of ways: boiled in spiced vinegar, they make a superb relish and can otherwise be used in cooking in place of some of the other suggestions made for certain recipes. Of course, their best-known use is in the making of wine, but there are many other fruits that can be turned into an alcoholic drink.

Liqueurs, Wines and Punches

Country wine is made from the flowers, berries, leaves and roots of plants that grow wild. The purest and most perfect of them are easily made and with the simplest and cheapest of equipment. To make elderflower wine, for example, you would need only florets (how many depends on the strength of flavour you like in your wine), boiling water, dried yeast, a quantity of sugar and assorted fermentation jars, bottles, a funnel, some tubing with which to siphon off the wine, a plastic bucket with a lid and the patience to wait a year whilst it matures.

The only limit to making a good liqueur from what is available in the countryside is your imagination. Almost anything can be used, but the most popular are those made from sloes (fruits of the blackthorn), wild damsons and cherries, and blackberries. The spirit is usually gin or brandy, although vodka and those lethal spirits that you brought back from holiday and now sit lurking at the very back of the drinks cabinet can also be used to good effect!

The simplest method is to place fruit, sugar and alcohol into a Kilner jar or similar container with an airtight lid. Place it on a windowsill and shake it daily for about a month before straining, bottling and storing in a cool place for a few months more. Extra flavours can be gained by using honey instead of sugar or adding herbs such as marjoram and spices such as nutmeg, ginger or cinnamon. Use 'chunks' or grated, rather than powder, as it is impossible to strain out the powder, which will add an unpleasant sawdusty taste and feel when it is drunk.

Classic Sloe Gin

Pick the sloes in the autumn, but don't worry about the traditionalists who insist that the fruit should not be picked until it has had a frost on it – it makes no difference at all to the end product. Again, according to the traditionalists, each sloe must be pricked with a fork, but that is very time-consuming and tedious, and I find that it is easiest to bruise them and split the skin by using the end of a wooden rolling pin. Alternatively, freeze them for a few days, after which time the skins will have burst.

450g/1lb sloes
225g/8oz castor or brown sugar
1 bottle gin (use the strongest proof you can find)

Place the prepared sloes into a wide-necked screw-top glass container, add the sugar and the gin and screw the lid on tightly. Shake daily for a few days, every other day for a few more and then once a week for a couple of months. Sloe gin made in early October should be ready to drink by Christmas, but the longer you keep it, the better it will be. Make Blackberry Brandy using the same method, except that it is obviously not necessary to prick the fruit.

Shooter's Punch

Punches should be served very hot and are usually made up of a mixture of wine and spirit. Although the ingredients here cannot be sourced free and from the countryside, it is exactly the sort of drink to welcome guests with before they sit down to one of the many game recipes from this book.

2 bottles claret
115ml/¼pt brandy
1 orange stuck with cloves
1 lemon, sliced
55g/2oz blanched whole almonds
55g/2oz raisins
115g/4oz sugar
cinnamon stick

Bake the orange in a medium oven for about an hour. Meanwhile, put the bottles of wine, the lemon, cinnamon stick, almonds, raisins and 55g/2ozs of the sugar into a saucepan. Add the orange when baked and simmer the pan uncovered for 15 minutes. Remove the cinnamon stick and transfer the punch into a suitable serving bowl.

In a smaller pan, place the remaining sugar and the brandy. Heat very gently, ignite with a match and, whilst still flaming, pour it into the punch bowl.

Wood for the Barbecue

Chestnut coppiced wood is often used to turn into barbecue charcoal; to make it yourself can be a long complicated process, involving smouldering fires and stacking timber into a pyramid. There is, however, no reason why, to add flavour to your game cookery, you should not add a few chips of oak, alder, apple or cherry wood to shop-bought charcoal a few minutes before the meat is due to finish cooking.

It is a good fire-base that ensures the success or otherwise of a barbecued meal – cooking over an open flame only gives raw meat a singed surface, whereas charcoal burning grey but shot with a reddish glow will give a constant heat and an evenly cooked meal. Only use as much charcoal as is required: there is often a tendency to totally fill the bottom of the barbecue, but this is not necessary unless a very large cooking surface is required.

Light the barbecue well in advance of the time that you wish to begin cooking – depending on the wind conditions and the likely draught, an hour ahead is not too early. The heat should be even and glowing before you even think to begin cooking. Low heat can be gained by spacing out the charcoal and a hot one by flicking away the white ash from the top of the charcoal. Always add fuel from the edge of the fire rather than tipping it on top of the burning charcoal, and if unwanted flames occur as a result of dripping fat, use a fine water spray or lay a damp lettuce leaf over the flames.

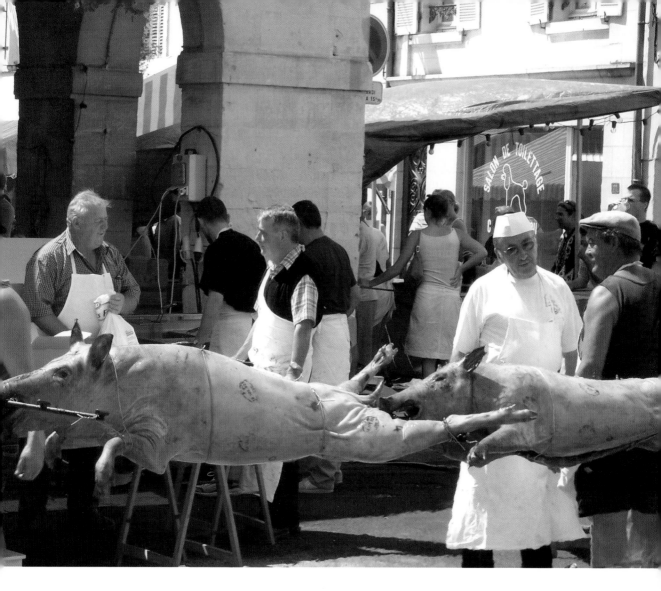

If you're feeling ambitious and wish to attempt a spit-roast over a bonfire, the same cooking principles apply, but using bags of shop-bought fuel would be financially prohibitive. Use well-dried, well-seasoned wood instead. Ash will burn well, as will oak if cut into small enough pieces – because of the high concentration of tannin in the latter, this will impart a delightful oaky taste to the meat that is being cooked. Some woods spit more than others so be sure to keep children and guests well away from the fire. For this reason, don't be tempted into using pine; it could also taint the meat with its natural turpentine fragrance.

Trimmings and Accompaniments

I eat my peas with honey; I've done it all my life. It makes the peas taste funny, But it keeps them on the knife (Anon.)

The pleasure of eating doesn't just begin when we sit at the table. There is the anticipation of the menu and, in some cases, knowing that we are about to cook what we have shot or caught ourselves, we are also given the opportunity to re-live that special day by the river, the partridge flying high and fast over a hedgerow or the autumn stalk in search of a deer.

A meal begins in its preparation – who has not suddenly felt hungry upon entering a kitchen and smelling onions and garlic being fried gently in butter? Perhaps, however, of all the senses, it is sight that provides the biggest 'turn on' – at least until such time as we can actually get to taste what is on the plate.

I forget who it was said that we eat with our eyes, but never has anything been more true. A piece of fish served on a white plate with mashed potatoes and cauliflower might taste OK, but it is not visually exciting. Put a salmon steak on the same white plate, pour over a delicately coloured lemon sauce that contains a few chopped pieces of chives and accompany it with fresh garden peas and the same meal already begins to take on new dimensions.

When planning a meal for guests, I always imagine the colours of everything on the plate before I make a decision as to what trimmings and accompaniments will best suit my purpose. For the same reason, take some time in choosing what crockery best suits your intended menu: too rich and deep a pattern can swamp the colours of the meal. Of course, it is not possible to have a different set of plates to compliment every single recipe, but it is a general point well worth bearing in mind. Size too matters: a vast array of food cramped on a small plate can be over-bearing and is certainly not as visually attractive – no matter how spectacular its contents are to taste. Big and plain seems to be the order of the day as far as choosing plates most suitable for the game cook.

VEGETABLES

Without imagination, vegetables can be a bit boring and a dish of overcooked, discoloured, tired-looking and watery mush can take many of us back to childhood days when a parent or teacher would say, 'Eat up your greens – they're good for you'. How often did we try to disguise them with gravy, sauce, just about anything to force them down! Well, as we all now know, overcooked vegetables were not, in fact, good for us, as the cooking (generally 'death by boiling') destroyed all the essential vitamins.

Some fish and game recipes suggest the type of sauce accompaniments designed to bring out the flavour of the flesh and it would be a shame to confuse your taste buds by adding extra unnecessary sauces to any vegetable dishes served with them. Steamed and *al dente*, the traditional seasonal types such as potatoes, carrots, cauliflower, broccoli, peas, beans, leeks, spinach (perfect with fish) and asparagus, are all that are needed to accompany a carefully prepared main course, but on occasions, where something a little different is required or when imagination is lacking, some of the following suggestions may be of help. Unless otherwise stated, all quantities are given to serve four people.

Parsnip and Apple Mash

This makes a delicious change from conventional mashed potato.

Peel 750g/1lb 10oz of floury potatoes such as Maris Piper and 225g/8oz of parsnips. Cut them into even-sized chunks and boil in two separate pans for 15–20 minutes until tender – adding a large eating apple that has been peeled, cored and cubed, to the parsnip pan for the final 5 minutes. Drain both pans well before adding the parsnips to the potatoes and stir over a low heat just long enough to drive off any moisture still remaining. Remove from heat, mash with butter in the normal way and then blend in 2 tablespoons of crème fraîche, and 2 tablespoons each of chopped fresh parsley and chopped fresh chives. Keep hot until ready to serve.

Turnip and Tarragon Rôsti

This makes a good accompaniment to a haunch of venison, joint of wild boar, ostrich steak or, in fact, almost any game-textured meat.

Peel 285g/10oz of turnip and 140g/5oz of potatoes, and grate on the largest holes. Mix both together in a bowl and stir in 15g/½oz of chopped tarragon, together with a generous pinch of seasoning.

In a heavy-bottomed frying pan (it needs to go in the oven, so make sure it is 'fit for purpose'), heat 55g/2oz of butter and 1 tablespoon of olive oil until the butter is frothing, then swirl it around the pan before laying in the grated mixture and firming it down (gently) with either a palette knife or the back of a wooden spoon. Occasionally work round the edges of the frying pan with a knife and cook on a medium heat for around 10 minutes (with a lid on) or until you see the edges beginning to brown. Lightly oil a plate big enough to hold the rôsti, hold it over the pan, flip the pan over and then slide the rôsti back into the pan so that the browned side is now facing upwards. Return to the heat for a further 5–10 minutes (no lid this time), then put it on the bottom of a pre-heated oven, gas mark 7, 220°C/425°F for about half an hour.

Parsnips in Batter

This recipe also makes a change from the normal – and you get to combine your veggies with a sort of Yorkshire pudding!

Peel 4–6 parsnips and discard any particularly 'woody' sections before cutting them into chunks and blanching in boiling water for 1–2 minutes. Dry, then toss them in a frying pan, to which 30g/1oz of fat and a dessertspoon of honey have been added. Turn frequently, making sure that all sides of the parsnips have been coated. Grease 10–12 patty tins, before making a batter as follows. Sieve 140g/5oz of plain flour into a bowl and add salt and pepper plus a pinch of mustard. Make a well in the centre, and add 2 eggs and 280ml/½pt of milk, beating thoroughly until a smooth batter is achieved.

Divide the parsnips into the patty tins, pour on the batter, and bake for 15–20 minutes at gas mark 7, 220°C (425°F).

Bubble and Squeak

For some reason, good old Bubble and Squeak goes well with any game dish. Mash your boiled potatoes with a little butter, but do not add any milk or cream as you perhaps would normally. Quickly boil some chopped cabbage or Brussels sprouts until they are cooked but still recognizably green (as Bubble and Squeak is a traditional method of using up leftovers, cold vegetables from a previous meal will do) and drain well. Fry 2 large onions in 30g/1oz butter until they are soft yet not discoloured and add them to the mashed potatoes, together with the greens. Reheat your frying pan and add a further 30g/1oz of butter. Tip in the Bubble and Squeak mix, flatten into a rough pancake shape and fry for a couple of minutes, or until the base is golden brown before turning and repeating the process on the other side (to turn the mix over, use the plate method as described above for Turnip and Tarragon Rôsti).

You could use the same mix to make several small cakes about 1–2cm/½–¾in thick rather than one large pancake shape.

Spring Onion Potato Cakes

Follow the above principles, but use a large bunch of finely chopped spring onions in place of the 2 onions and omit the cabbage or Brussels sprouts. All potato cakes should be dusted with a little flour before being pan-fried. Once cooked, the cakes can be set to one side and baked in the oven when required.

French Mix Vegetables

Joints of rabbit, quarters or halves of game birds and similar, can be very successfully braised or pot-roasted. The meat is first of all browned with the aid of a little fat or oil and then placed on a bed of vegetables in a casserole dish or pan (which must have a tightly fitting lid). Rather than merely using chopped vegetables as a base, a French Mix makes the dish a lot more interesting.

On a board, chop or slice 2 carrots, 1 large onion, 2 cloves of garlic, 2 large tomatoes (these can be omitted if, like many people, you or your guests are not fans of cooked tomatoes) and some parsley (with the stalk removed). Heat a tablespoon of olive oil in the pan, put in the onions, season with a little sea salt and freshly ground pepper and sweat over a low heat before adding the remaining ingredients. Rest the meat on the French Mix and add a splash of white wine or just enough stock to prevent burning. Cover the pan and cook very gently until the meat is done. Times will obviously vary depending on the type, joint and quality of the meat being used.

As this is basically a steaming method (unless it is pot-roasted, in which case, no liquid is added and it is cooked in the oven), there is no reason why the same method should not be adapted for a whole trout or some of the firmer-fleshed fish and the cooking time reduced.

Game Chips

You cannot have a game cookery book that doesn't contain a recipe for Game Chips. Here is ours.

Serves 4–6

Peel and slice (very thinly) around 700g/1½lb of potatoes. Place them in a colander and run the cold tap over them in order to remove any excess starch, then dry the slices on kitchen roll. Heat some oil in a chip pan and add the potatoes, a few slices at a time. Fry until crisp and golden brown. Once done, remove any excess fat by placing the chips on more kitchen roll and place them in the bottom of a reasonably hot oven to keep them warm until ready for serving

DUMPLINGS
Dumplings are always good with a casserole and together they make the ideal winter 'comfort' food.

Bread Dumplings

These are a little different to the normal suet variety and are easily made.

In a saucepan, sauté 1 tablespoon of chopped onion in 2 tablespoons of butter until golden. Stir in 2 cups of whole-wheat breadcrumbs (soaked in water and squeezed dry), together with a teaspoon of salt. Remove the pan from the heat and cool the mixture. Stir in 2 eggs, ½ cup of cracker biscuit crumbs, 1 teaspoon of chopped parsley and a pinch each of paprika, nutmeg and ginger before stirring well. Shape the mixture into balls and add to the stew or casserole for about the last 15–20 minutes of its scheduled cooking time. If the mixture is too crumbly to shape, add a few drops of water or olive oil.

Mushroom Dumplings

Lightly fry 225g/8oz of very finely chopped mushrooms with one finely chopped onion before mixing them in a bowl with 115g/4oz of white breadcrumbs, 2 tablespoons of chopped parsley, 1 dessertspoon of tomato purée and an egg. Bind the mixture together well before shaping it into small balls (if you use about a tablespoon of mixture for each ball, you should end up with 12–14 miniature dumplings). Coat each one with flour, then brown in hot oil in a frying pan. When well seared, add to the stew or casserole for the last 20–30 minutes of cooking.

STUFFINGS

Traditionally, stuffing is placed in the body cavity of the bird, but it is far better to stuff a bird intended for roasting from the neck end. Push as much stuffing as possible in the cavity formed between the skin and the flesh of the breast. Bake any remaining stuffing in a dish in the oven and serve as a further accompaniment.

Fish should be stuffed in the body cavity in the normal way. Don't forget that stuffing any meat or fish will increase cooking times.

Cranberry Stuffing

This goes well with duck, grouse or goose. Make it by sweating off a small, finely chopped onion in about 30g/1oz of butter. Once the onion has softened, stir in 125g/6oz of freshly grated brown bread-crumbs, 125g/4oz of cranberries, 1 tablespoon of chopped parsley and ¼ teaspoon of ground mixed spice. Season with salt and pepper, bind the whole together with a beaten egg and leave to cool before stuffing the bird in the usual way.

Apple and Herb Stuffing

Sweat off a small onion in the manner described above. Remove from the heat, allow to cool and then stir in a peeled, chopped and cored cooking apple, 55g/2oz of fresh white breadcrumbs, 1 table-spoon each of chopped parsley and thyme, the grated zest of a lemon and salt and pepper to season. Bind all together with a beaten egg and leave until completely cold.

Chestnut Stuffing

This is a classic for any game bird. The following recipe appears in *The Game Book* by Carolyn Little (The Crowood Press, 1988; paperback edition, 1998).

Take 1kg/2lb 3oz of chestnuts and make a small slit in the chestnut skins with a sharp knife. Place them in a pan and cover with a mixture of one part milk to three parts water. Boil for 20 minutes. Drain the nuts into a colander and run the tap over them until they are cool. Remove the skins and mash the chestnuts well before putting them into a pan containing 275ml/½pt of game stock (*see* Chapter 15). Simmer until tender. Season with salt, pepper and a pinch of cinnamon or nutmeg. Add a teaspoon of castor sugar and bind the whole together with the aid of 55g/2oz of warm butter.

Spinach and Mushroom Stuffing

Try this with wild boar loin chops. The fact that it is served in triangular cake-like wedges makes it an interesting and unusual accompaniment.

NB Unless you are absolutely positive of a correct identification, it is dangerous to risk using any mushrooms picked from the wild.

Heat a tablespoon of oil in a heavy-bottomed pan and add a large chopped onion. Cover and cook for around 15 minutes or until the onion is soft. Having roughly sliced 140g/5oz of mushrooms, and be as adventurous as you like with whatever types are available from the greengrocers, add them to the onion base and fry them for 2–3 minutes. Then add 225g/8oz of young spinach leaves and cook only until they begin to wilt. Add 115g/4oz of freshly grated breadcrumbs, season and mix well.

Heat a little oil in a small non-stick frying pan and put the stuffing mix into this, pressing it down firmly (use a wooden spoon) so that the mixture forms a thick pancake. Fry the underside until it is crisp and golden coloured. Remove from the hob and grate a thin layer of cheese over the top before placing the pan under the grill for a few minutes in order to brown off the top. Turn out onto a plate and cut into wedges. Experiment with different types of cheese.

Lemon and Mushroom Stuffing

Trout is simplicity itself to bake – all you really need to do is to gut and clean it, wrap it in foil together with a knob of butter and some fennel and place it in the oven for about 15–25 minutes (depending on its size) at gas mark 4, 180°C/350°F. However, for a little extra taste, try this Lemon and Mushroom Stuffing.

Take 115g/4oz of sliced button mushrooms, 2 chopped shallots, 4 tablespoons of white wine vinegar and the grated zest and juice of a lemon. Strip the leaves from the stalks of about half-a-dozen sprigs of parsley and thyme and, in a bowl, combine all the ingredients before finally seasoning with salt and black pepper. Stuff the fish and bake in the normal way.

SALADS

Salads can be a good accompaniment to many situations: just two examples are when using any left-over cold game as lunch or a starter, or to complement a simple meal of wild fish. Salad recipes are numerous and not really within the scope of this book, but I thought it interesting to describe a Classic Green Salad as prepared by our French neighbours and also to include a tried and tested favourite – Rice and Orange.

Classic Green Salad

Use any combination of these ingredients: lettuce, chicory, endives, sorrel, garden cress, watercress, young spinach, chard, very young dandelion leaves (the older ones are too bitter unless stood in old water overnight), nasturtium leaves, cucumber, celery, Chinese cabbage, the green tops of chives, spring onions and shallots. Herbs can include parsley, tarragon and chervil.

Wash all ingredients and dry thoroughly, using a wire salad basket or salad spinner (I always keep my spinner in the fridge, as this is probably the best place to store prepared salad ingredients for the longest period of time). Shred the greens with your fingers, rather than cut them with a knife, as they tend to 'bruise' less this way.

The French insist that a wooden salad bowl is best, the inside of which should first be rubbed with a cut clove of garlic. Place any dressing at the bottom of the bowl before adding the salad ingredients, but *do not* toss them until immediately before serving, otherwise the leaves will begin to wilt. Traditionally, salad servers must be placed crossed and resting over the rim of the bowl.

RICE

Obviously rice would be a natural accompaniment to fish, salads and curried game dishes, but it makes a perfect foil for all kinds of game, especially if you can find the type known as Camargue rice, which, with its slightly nutty flavour and when combined with wild mushrooms, goes particularly well with pigeon recipes. As its name suggests, it comes from the southern region of France, but is nowadays available in the UK. If you cannot find a source near you, try a substitute of mixed long-grain and wild rice instead.

Rice and Orange Salad

This salad complements the flavour of cold meat and is perfect in the summer months – it is also simple to prepare!

Serves 4

Boil 225g/8oz of long grain rice and allow to cool. Peel, segment and finely chop 2 oranges, carefully removing all the pith and stones. Slice a quarter in half lengthways and, with a teaspoon, scrape out and discard the seeds. Cube a cucumber and mix it together with the rice and the orange before seasoning well and adding 3 tablespoons of French dressing. Mix again and chill for an hour before serving.

Risotto with Fresh Asparagus and Mushrooms

This rich risotto makes an ideal accompaniment or starter if you wish, for an Italian-themed dinner party. Like all risottos it is so versatile that it can also be used as a midweek supper dish and is complete in itself. Feel free to do what they do in the Venice region, where risottos are said to have originated – no doubt following the return of Silk Road adventurers who had seen what the Chinese could do with rice. Venetians or inhabitants of the Po Valley in Italy will argue for many hours about the relative merits of Carnaroli, Vialone or Arborio rice but then choose just about any ingredients to hand for their risotto's main flavours. Here we use a pheasant stock base with asparagus spears and mushrooms.

Serves 4
10 stalks asparagus
small handful button mushrooms, washed and sliced
340g/12oz Arborio rice
1.1ltr/2pt pheasant or any other game-based stock
1 medium onion, finely chopped
45g/1½oz butter
1 glass dry white wine
small fistful grated Reggio Parmagiano or other hard Italian cheese

Prepare the asparagus by boiling for 3–5 minutes, depending on thickness, and removing from the pan whilst just cooked but firm. Lightly fry the sliced button mushrooms in oil until just golden. Set aside. Take a heavy-based pan, not too big, and sauté the onions slowly in the butter until soft, but do not allow them to brown – this will take 5–10 minutes and should not be hurried. Now add the rice, allowing this to become coated in the butter, say 2–3 minutes. Again, it must not brown so ideally stay with the risotto and get your guests to come and talk to you in the kitchen. Now pour in the glass of wine and allow this to evaporate on a low heat, which will take another few minutes. From this point, the risotto should cook for a further 18 minutes. Pour on a third of the stock and allow this to simmer away. Add the remaining stock gradually until at the end the whole litre is absorbed; the risotto should never be allowed to become dry. At the end of the cooking time, pour off any surplus liquid, depending on how dry or moist you like your risotto. Stir in the asparagus, mushrooms and grated cheese. Test for seasoning, although it probably won't need any. Cover and leave to rest for 2 minutes before serving.

HERBS

Talking of subtlety in any form of cooking, but especially in connection with game, herbs are an essential part of almost every recipe and suggestion. They differ from vegetables in that they should merely add a suggestion of flavour rather than being a dish in their own and so it is up to the cook to decide how best to use them in marinades, sauces and stocks.

For the serious chef, it may pay to consider the possibilities of growing one's own. Most small gardens have space for a few herbs and even those without any garden at all can grow some in pots on a patio or in a window box. Herbs likely to be of most use to the game cook include: basil, bay, chives, dill, fennel, garlic, mint, parsley, rosemary, sage, tarragon and thyme.

Growing

Many herbs are Mediterranean in origin and, therefore, do well in a drained and sheltered location. Some are half-hardy and will need winter protection, whilst others, such as chives, die back in the autumn but, provided that they've been regularly fed and watered the previous summer, will reappear the following spring. You can try and keep them growing during the winter by potting up a clump and bringing it indoors.

Most can be raised from seed, but as the young plants can be bought cheaply from a garden centre, there is little point in doing so – beware of the puny varieties often sold in supermarkets, which may last no longer than a week. Once they are established, you can take cuttings from some of the woody types, such as rosemary and sage: this is best done in the autumn.

Drying for Winter Use

During the growing season, you will normally pick herbs as and when they are needed. For winter use, however, you may need to dry them – and most herbs can be dried. Do this by hanging them in bunches or laying them out on a tray in the sunshine (in the absence of sunshine, dry them in an oven which has recently been used for cooking and is, therefore, warm but switched off). After a couple of days in the sun, leave them at room temperature for 2 weeks, but turn them regularly until they are crisp and flaky. The leaves can then be crushed and stored in airtight containers until required.

GARNISHES, CHUTNEYS AND JELLIES

As mentioned at the beginning of this chapter, eating is as much about looking at a meal as it is about tasting it, but both senses can be enhanced with a little, sometimes literal, dressing. A few aromatic herbs sprinkled here, an eye-catching sprig of watercress there; a jar of raspberry or redcurrant jelly for serving alongside grouse, venison or boar – all these can make a difference and are well worth the effort.

Garnish of Young Turnip Leaves

Young turnip leaves can be used as a garnish over roasted vegetables. Wash them and, while they are still wet, fry them in 1 tablespoon of olive oil, together with a crushed clove of garlic. Once the leaves have wilted, sprinkle them with a tablespoon of water and cook gently until the water has evaporated.

Green Mayonnaise

This goes well with a simply baked trout. Place 2 egg yolks, ½ teaspoon of dried mustard powder, salt and pepper into a bowl and beat until it has just begun to thicken slightly. Very carefully begin adding a few drops of olive oil to the mixture while beating constantly. When it has thickened sufficiently, beat in a few drops of lemon juice or white wine vinegar until a tablespoon has been added in total. Fold in 2 tablespoons of finely chopped parsley and 1 tablespoon each of finely chopped watercress and chives. Chill before serving. To avoid the notorious problems involved in creating a mayonnaise, it is possible to cheat by adding the herbs to a proprietary ready-made brand.

SOME QUICK SUGGESTIONS

- Use garlic dressing with game such as grilled pheasant and salad.
- Garnish fish with watercress and a thick slice of lemon and use wild rocket with a partridge risotto.
- Have a jar of mango chutney to hand with a recipe containing hare, and pickled red cabbage when serving pigeon.
- Serve goose with the sauces, stuffings and garnishes normally reserved for the Christmas turkey.
- Add a swirl of cream to soup and top it off with flaked almonds or croutons.
- As an alternative to Game Chips, garnish a dish with root vegetable crisps, available from many supermarkets.
- Accompanying your meal with bread – and not just when eating soup or eating pâtés and terrines, but at any time as the French do – also adds to the 'wholesomeness' of many a recipe. There are plenty of varieties to choose from: traditional French bread makes an ideal accompaniment to terrines; garlic bread with a spicy game soup.

Marinades, Sauces and Stocks

Recipe for sauce to wildfowl:

Port wine, or claret	1 glass
Sauce à la Russe (the older the better)	1 tablespoonful
Catsup	1 ditto
Lemon juice	1 ditto
Lemon peel	1 slice
Shallot (large)	1, cut in slices
Cayenne (the darkest, not that like brick dust)	4 grains
Mace	1 or 2 blades

To be scalded, strained, and added to the mere gravy, which comes from the bird in roasting. To complete this, the fowl should be cut up in a silver dish, that has a lamp under it, while the sauce is simmering with it.

(Col. Peter Hawker, *Instructions to Young Sportsmen*; 1814)

MARINADES

Marinades help to breakdown meat fibres as well as imbibing them with subtle tastes. They also counteract the possibility of dryness as the meat cooks. Meat joints should be left in a marinade for at least 12 hours in order to bring out the best flavours. Remember to turn the meat occasionally during that time. It may be that some joints and whole game birds are too big to be totally immersed in a marinade – unless you were to mix up such a quantity that it would become very expensive and wasteful. In such cases, the easiest way of ensuring that the meat has received its full share of marinade is to place it and the mixture into a strong plastic bag and securely tie the neck. Then, it is a simple matter to periodically turn the bag over.

There is no exact science to preparing a marinade and a typical one that will work well with heavier meats such as boar, hare, venison or goose is likely to combine some or all of the following ingredients:

1 bottle red wine (full-bodied rather than the lighter Gamay grape type)
2 tablespoons red wine vinegar (or rather less of balsamic)
chopped onion and garlic
herbs

pinch mixed dried spices
pinch grated nutmeg
1 or 2 bay leafs
2 'glugs' olive oil
6 juniper berries, if you can get them

There is, however, a school of thought amongst some professional chefs that the wine only serves to pickle the meat and in doing so, actually draws out some of the moisture. You may prefer to follow their advice and omit all but the slightest amount of wine, replacing it with rather more olive oil.

Ginger and Garlic Marinade

For lighter meats such as partridge and rabbit, this marinade gives an almost oriental combination, especially if a small amount of soy sauce is added.

Combine together one finely chopped onion, two crushed cloves of garlic and a tablespoon of freshly grated ginger plus 2 teaspoons of chopped parsley. Add liquid consisting of ¼ cup of lemon juice, the same of sesame oil, two tablespoons of soy sauce and the same of honey. Not only will this make an excellent marinade but the mixture can also be brushed over meat when grilling or barbecuing.

SAUCES

Some sauce recipes take, as their base, either a hollandaise or white cream sauce. With care, both are easy to make.

Hollandaise Sauce

Divide 115g/4oz of butter into three parts. Into the top of a double saucepan (*bain marie*), or use a Pyrex-type bowl over a pan of hot but not boiling water, place 4 egg yolks and one part of the butter. Stir rapidly and continuously until the butter is melted and add the second knob of butter. As the sauce thickens and the butter melts, add the third piece of butter, all the time stirring incessantly and keeping the water just below boiling point. When the butter is melted and the sauce is well mixed, remove from the source of heat and continue beating for at least a couple of minutes. Add 2 teaspoons of lemon juice or vinegar and a pinch of white pepper and salt. Replace the pan or bowl over the hot, but not boiling, water for another minute or two, all the time stirring constantly with the wooden spoon. Remove from the heat and use as required. Should the mixture curdle, immediately beat in a tablespoon of boiling water, which will have the effect of rebinding the emulsion.

Cream or White Sauce

Melt 2 tablespoons of butter over a low heat and gradually add the same of flour, stirring constantly for 3–5 minutes until a roux is formed. Gradually add about a cup of milk or cream, still stirring well in order to blend well. Season to taste and continue cooking until the sauce has thickened to the required consistency.

Brown Sauce

Several game recipes call for a base of Brown Sauce. You could cheat and experiment by including a proprietary brand such as Daddy's Sauce or similar and, provided that the variety is not too 'hot' or spicy, there is no reason why it should not work well. To make a simple, homemade brown sauce, however, is not too difficult.

In a saucepan melt 1½ tablespoons of butter and gradually add 1½ tablespoons of flour. Cook slowly over a low heat, stirring occasionally until this roux is thoroughly blended and slightly brown in colour (this will occur more rapidly if one browns a few pieces of onion in the butter before adding the flour). Moisten gently with 2 cups of stock or beef consommé (the latter can be bought in tins and will be found in the 'soup' section at the supermarket), bring to the boil and cook for 3–5 minutes, stirring continuously. Lower the heat and simmer gently for a further 30 minutes before skimming off the fat and straining the sauce through a fine sieve.

Sweet Sauce

It is traditional to serve sweet sauces with game. This one is slightly unusual in the fact that it equally complements any cold meat and is also perfect when used as a topping for ice cream – yes, really!

Take approximately 170g/6oz of butter and melt it gently in a heavy-bottomed saucepan. Add ½ teaspoon of nutmeg, 1 teaspoon of freshly grated ginger, ¼ cup of roughly chopped pistachio nuts and ½ cup of brown sugar before heating for about a minute. Gradually stir in about ¼ cup of dark rum and a further ¼ cup of brandy and simmer over a very low heat until all the ingredients have combined. Pour into a sauceboat and serve straight away.

Creamed Apple Sauce

Still on the alcohol theme, this sauce makes a great accompaniment to game, wildfowl and wild boar.

Melt around 115g/4oz of butter in a pan before adding 2 peeled, cored and sliced eating apples. Once these have softened, add a cup of stock – if you've none of your own to hand, made-up chicken cubes or granules will suffice – together with 2 tablespoons of freshly chopped tarragon. Simmer over a low heat for a couple of minutes and then begin including 1 cup of cider, ½ cup of white dessert wine and ¼ cup of apple brandy. When all is gently simmering, finally stir in ½ cup of double cream and serve immediately.

It is important to remember that the idea of adding alcohol to sauces is not to get your guests 'sloshed', but to enhance the sauce with a subtle flavour. When cooked for long enough, all the alcohol will have evaporated and it is essential that it has – otherwise it will leave a sharp and bitter taste.

Raisin Sauce

There are many sauces that contain raisins but I don't think any Raisin Sauce can be much simpler to make than this one, which we have modified from a recipe I was given by a French neighbour.

Into a bowl, place 3 tablespoons of dark brown sugar and a tablespoon of Dijon mustard. Mix in 3 tablespoons of red wine vinegar and stir until all the sugar has dissolved. Next, put the sauce into a heavy-bottomed saucepan, add a cup of brown sauce (*see* above) and simmer on a minimum heat for around 10 minutes. Whilst the sauce is doing its stuff in the pan, soak approximately ¼–½ cup of raisins in hot brandy for the same length of time. At the end of the 10 minutes, drain the raisins and add them to the contents of the saucepan before simmering for a further 5 minutes and serving hot.

Staffordshire Venison Sauce

Brown sauce is also used in the making of this sauce, which, surprise, surprise, goes well with venison!

In the top half of a double saucepan (or in a heat-proof bowl placed over a pan of boiling water), combine 4 tablespoons of brown sauce, ½ cup of port, the same of mushroom purée (or mushroom ketchup, if you can get it), a scant teaspoon of sugar, a tablespoon of lemon juice and a generous pinch of cayenne pepper. Stir frequently until all the ingredients are blended, but do not let the sauce itself boil. One advantage of this particular sauce is that it can be kept in the fridge (in a sealed jar) for at least a week.

Sauce Rouenaise

For wild goose or duck why not make a Sauce Rouenaise? If you have saved the livers from any game birds during the season, you can use two or three in this recipe.

Put ½ cup of red wine, 5 peppercorns, 1 bay leaf, ½ teaspoon of thyme and 2 finely chopped shallots in a saucepan and bring to the boil, cooking until the ingredients have reduced by around two-thirds. Add 2 tablespoons of brown sauce and bring back to the boil before removing the pan from the heat. Finely chop the livers and add them to the sauce (the residual heat will cook them). Finally, push the complete sauce through a sieve and add a dash of cognac before serving.

Marsala Sauce

This sauce goes very well with pheasant and partridge breasts. Make it by adding crushed juniper berries, chopped prunes, chopped onion and celery to some previously prepared game stock and cooking until tender. Sieve the sauce, add a large glass of Marsala wine and thicken the sauce with a little cornflour, at the same time adding any juices from the meat, which by this stage, would have been cooked and resting.

Onion and Lemon Sauce

Again, this is a very useful accompaniment to all manner of small game or even joints of wild boar. Simmer 1.2ltr/2pt of game stock, to which the juice and rind of a lemon has been added, in a pan. At the same time, in a second pan, sweat 170g/6oz chopped spring onions in about 55g/2oz of butter – using only the white parts rather than the green-tipped leaves. After they have softened, remove with a slotted spoon and put to one side. Add 55g/2oz of flour to the juices that remain in the pan and make a *roux* before gradually mixing in and continually stirring the sieved game/lemon juice stock. Once a smooth sauce occurs, add a pinch of cayenne pepper and a little salt to taste, before covering the pan and leaving to simmer gently for 10 minutes. Add the spring onions and simmer for a further 10 minutes or until the sauce has turned smooth and velvety in both look and texture. Pour over the cooked game birds or joint and serve immediately.

Lemon Sauce

Any type of lemon sauce is perfect with fish. This particular recipe combines wine, honey and soy sauce to make an unusual and delightful accompaniment, especially when poured over fish that has been grilled or barbecued.

Heat 1 tablespoon of good quality olive oil in a heavy-bottomed saucepan before adding 1 teaspoon of freshly grated ginger and ½ a finely chopped lemon (include the peel and zest) and sauté for a minute. Then stir in ½ cup of chicken stock; the same amount of dry white wine; a ¼ cup of lemon juice and 1 tablespoon of honey. Simmer gently for around 10 minutes before finally adding a teaspoon of soy sauce and serving hot.

One great advantage of this recipe is that the sauce can be kept in the fridge for up to 2 days and reheated over a low heat prior to serving.

Aromatic Sauce

This is another hot sauce suitable for fish, especially salmon steaks.

Bring a cupful of fish stock to the boil and add a pinch of crushed thyme and a small pinch each of basil, marjoram and sage. Remove the saucepan from the heat and add a teaspoon each of finely chopped chives and finely chopped shallots, a few grains of nutmeg and 3 coarsely ground peppercorns. Season to taste, cover the pan and allow the mixture to infuse for 15 minutes. Blend together a teaspoon each of butter and flour over a medium heat, add the strained infusion, and boil for a further 5 minutes. Add 1 tablespoon of lemon juice and 1 tablespoon each of freshly chopped parsley and tarragon. Serve immediately.

Cucumber Cream Sauce

Again suitable for fish.

To a cup of white sauce (*see* above), add a ½ cup of grated cucumber pulp or thinly sliced cucumber, and a dash of cayenne pepper. Heat gently for 10 minutes, stirring regularly before serving straight away.

Figaro Sauce

Cold sauces can also work well with fish. Try this Figaro Sauce, which can actually also be used on cold game as well as fish.

To 1½ cups of hollandaise sauce (*see* above), add 3 tablespoons of tomato purée and a generous tablespoon of tomato paste, all the time beating well. Fold in a tablespoon of finely chopped parsley and season with a few grains of cayenne pepper and a little salt.

Samphire Sauce

This also makes an excellent accompaniment to any fish, but is particularly good with cold salmon and trout.

In a colander, rinse 2–3 handfuls of young samphire fronds under cold running water. Chop roughly and purée in a food processor before slowly adding 3 tablespoons of olive oil and a little seasoning. Transfer the purée to a mixing bowl and gently fold in 250ml/8fl oz of crème fraîche, lemon zest and a little lemon juice to taste.

Picada

In the border areas of France and Spain, residents there have what would appear to be a very unusual and tasty way of flavouring and thickening sauces intended for small game and rabbit. Known locally as Picada, this sauce contains a mixture of crushed pine nuts, walnuts, garlic, fried or toasted bread and a little lard, all of which are then combined with tomatoes and added to the meat whilst cooking.

Cream in Sauces

Some recipes include the use of double cream, but to use it successfully and without the risk of the cream curdling as it is added to the sauce, there are several points that must be remembered.

Double cream (single will not thicken) should be added to a very small quantity of liquid – normally, the deglazed (*see* Glossary) juices obtained from the roasting or cooking pan: by cooking it slowly and stirring continuously, it should eventually thicken, especially if it is being made in a roasting tin and not in a tall, narrow pan. To help prevent the possibility of the cream curdling as it is added to the deglazed mixture, the best chefs recommend that the cream should be at kitchen temperature rather than used straight from the fridge.

Clarified Butter

Yet other sauce recipes call for the use of clarified butter, and even if they don't, it is a good way of frying game bird breasts or fish when something simple is preferred. Perhaps the easiest way of turning 'normal' butter into clarified, is to place it in a dish in an oven set at the lowest temperature. After half an hour or so, the butter will have completely melted, leaving a sediment at the bottom of the dish. Very carefully, pour off the 'clear' butter into another dish, leaving the sediment at the base of the original container. Storage times for clarified butter are about a fortnight in the fridge and as much as 12 weeks if properly kept in plastic boxes in the freezer.

Sauce-Making in the Microwave

With a microwave, even some of the more temperamental sauces such as hollandaise can be made with less danger of the sauce curdling, and white sauces, based on flour and butter, are less likely to be lumpy. There is almost no risk of a sauce sticking to a pan and some can, in fact, be made in the sauce bowl or serving jug.

Despite being easier to make, they do, nevertheless, require frequent stirring (use a balloon whisk for white sauces), which helps prevent the sauce from cooking too quickly and also lessens the chance of lumps forming. Should a particular sauce show signs of curdling as it cooks, quickly open the door and start whisking manically, as this will arrest the cooking process until the problem can be solved.

NB Remember that microwave-cooked sauces continue to thicken during cooling.

Sauces that are reduced during cooking, so as to thicken them, should be cooked uncovered until reaching the desired thickness, stirring frequently with a wooden spoon. It will pay to use a large bowl for this in order to prevent splattering as the sauce begins to bubble.

Most sauces, even if not made in the microwave, can be successfully reheated in one. They should be loosely covered and all those containing cream should be reheated very gently, probably on a 'low' setting.

STOCKS

Like marinades, stock making is not an exact science and quantities of liquids and varieties of ingredients can be altered to suit. Therefore, do not be afraid to adapt any of the suggestions that follow. One word of warning: do not attempt to substitute ground black pepper in place of peppercorns, as prolonged cooking can turn ground black pepper bitter.

Jellied Stock

Sometimes stock is used when making a game pie to eat cold and it is necessary for a 'jelly' to set around the meat as the pie cools after cooking. Jellied stock is made by the same methods previously described, but only meat bones are used, due to them containing a high level of natural gelatine. Cracking or sawing in half any large bones before cooking will more easily release this gelatine and the best bones to use for this particular purpose are beef or veal.

Brown Stock

If you can get hold of some beef bones, place them together with a couple of sliced onions and carrots in a roasting tray or similar and brown the bones on all sides in a moderately hot oven. Transfer all to a large heavy-bottomed pan and add about 3.4ltr/6pt of water, ½ tablespoon of salt, a pinch of thyme, a bouquet garni and a couple of celery stalks.

Bring to the boil before turning down the heat and simmering for about 4 hours or until the stock has reduced by about a third. Skim off any accumulating fat as and when necessary throughout this period – use a large spoon or soak it up with kitchen roll: alternatively, let the stock cool and lift it off once it has formed a 'crust'. Eventually, strain the liquid through a sieve and store in the fridge (for up to a week) or freeze (for 2–3 months), ready to use in a brown sauce.

Fish Stock

If you're not too squeamish (you will need to remove gills and eyes!) and you have access to a regular supply of freshly caught fish, all the heads, bones and trimmings can be used to make fish stock. If your supply is, however, a little spasmodic, or you only want a fish stock for a special occasion or particular recipe, then the easiest thing to do is ask a fishmonger or the fish department of your local supermarket for the heads and trimmings of some lean white fish (turbot, monkfish and sole bones are, in the opinion of many chefs, the best). Wherever you source them, do not include any oily fish, as this may result in a bitter and unpleasant-tasting stock.

To make approximately 2ltr/3½pt, sweat 1 onion (or cloves of garlic if preferred), ½ fennel bulb, 1 leek and 2 celery sticks – all of which should be roughly chopped – in 55g/2oz butter, taking care not to allow the butter to burn, as this will colour the stock – the idea is to get it as 'clear'-looking as possible. Add the stalks of a sprig of fresh parsley, together with a bay leaf and 5–6 black pepper-corns. Next, put in the bones, heads, trimmings, and so on, of about 900g/2lb of fish and continue cooking on quite a high heat for a further few minutes before sloshing in about a ¼ bottle of dry white wine. Reduce the resultant mixture by boiling until almost all the liquid has disappeared and then add 2.25ltr/4pt of water. Simmer for 20 minutes before pouring and pushing the stock through a fine sieve (use the back of a wooden spoon). After cooling, it can be kept for 2–3 days in the fridge or, if divided into plastic airtight containers, for 1–2 months in the freezer.

If preferred, 2 tablespoons of olive oil can be used instead of butter and a further option is to add the juice of a lemon at the point at which water is introduced, but beware of including too many conflicting flavours, as the stock should add a subtle taste, rather than overpowering any sauce to which it is added.

Game Stock

This can be made from the fresh carcasses of game birds from which the breasts have been removed for another recipe or, if you have had a couple of roast birds, the left-over carcasses could also be used. Giblets can also be included or, if you have a regular supply of birds throughout the season, they can be made into a separate stock (*see* below).

Place two raw pheasant carcasses in a heavy-bottomed pan. Add half a garlic bulb, roughly crushed, 3–4 sticks of celery, 2 small leeks, 2 small onions and 2 medium-sized carrots, all of which should be roughly chopped. Also include 3 bay leaves and 3 sprigs each of fresh thyme, rosemary and parsley. Add 4–5 black peppercorns and approximately 4.50ltr/8pt of cold water. As with the brown stock above, bring to the boil before simmering gently for about 4 hours and skimming off the fat as it appears. Once the process is complete, empty the stock into storage containers via a fine sieve.

Giblet Stock

For a small quantity of giblet stock, place the necks, gizzards and hearts of 2 or 3 birds into a heavy-bottomed saucepan and add just enough olive oil to ensure that they are slightly browned without burning on the heat. Stir in 1ltr/1¾pt of water, bring to the boil and remove any residue floating on the surface before adding 1 chopped onion, a chopped celery stalk and a chopped carrot. Include a bouquet garni and 5 black peppercorns before simmering for about an hour. Like all the other stocks described above, it should finally be passed through a sieve before being cooled and can be stored in the fridge for up to a week or in the freezer for 2–3 months.

Helpful Hints

What Mrs Drydon, the family cook, didn't know about her subject was, as His Lordship was fond of saying, 'not damn well worth knowing'. Having been employed in the same kitchen for thirty years, she reckoned she'd cooked 'everything from snails to suckling pigs and a lot else in between.'
(John Forester, *A Little Country Knowledge*, 1879)

This chapter contains a few helpful hints and general observations, which, for one reason or another, have not been made elsewhere. Perhaps the most useful advice to give is that, apart from obviously ensuring that all recipes are prepared well, cooked safely and are, therefore, unlikely to cause you, your family or guests to suffer from an attack of food poisoning, cooking should always be a pleasure and an adventure.

Necessity has often been the mother of invention in the kitchen as much as it has elsewhere and so don't ever get too hung up on following a particular recipe to the letter. If it suggests using sage and you abhor sage, use thyme. If it says rum and you prefer brandy, use brandy – many a culinary masterpiece was invented because one ingredient was absent and another plentiful.

THE BURSA TEST

The best way to cook any game bird depends entirely on its age. Old birds will always benefit from a recipe that requires slow cooking, whilst young ones will make the best stir-fries.

There are many traditional ways of aging birds: looking at the length of spur on a cock pheasant, for example, or holding the bottom beak of a grouse between finger and thumb to see if it bends (if it does, then in all likelihood it is a young bird, if it remains firm, an old one). The Game Conservancy Trust (GCT) found, many years ago, that the Bursa Test was a reliable way of aging game birds once they were dead. You may, however, get some strange looks if you attempt to carry it out in front of an audience!

Young birds have a short passage, called the bursa, which is situated between the anus (vent) and tail. As a bird matures, the bursa passage shortens and may eventually disappear altogether. By inserting a matchstick into this passage and seeing how far it will go, will give away the bird's age. The distance for pheasant is 2.5cm/1in; for grouse and partridge, 1cm/½in. As far as I'm aware, science has yet to give measurements for a young ostrich!

HANGING GAME

Hanging game for a few days will increase the flavour and tenderize the meat. Just how long you hang it depends on how 'gamey' you like your meat to taste, what type of game you're hanging (a grouse, or instance, will taste much stronger after being hung for three days than will a pheasant or partridge given the same time) and the weather conditions (thundery weather can turn a bird rapidly, even if the temperature is not high). In warm weather, two or three days might be all that is required, but during an exceptionally cold period, a week or even up to ten days would not be too long. Find a cool place to hang your game and, in the early part of the season, drape them with muslin and secure with rubber bands if there are likely to be any flies around.

Traditionally, game birds are hung by their heads, whilst rabbits, hares and the carcasses of boar or venison are hung by their back legs, heads facing downwards. Hares are unusual in that they are normally hung with their guts still in, whereas rabbits, boar and deer have their intestines removed as soon as possible after being killed. Wild duck are not generally hung as, for some reason, the practice does not seem to improve their flavour, but if you have a particular yearning to do so, they, unlike pheasants and partridge, are normally hung by their feet. Pigeons are normally plucked, drawn and eaten whilst fresh and do not require hanging.

A word of warning: the longer game birds have been hung, the more likely you are to tear the skin when plucking.

TO PLUCK OR NOT TO PLUCK...

It is not always necessary to pluck game birds and if all that is required is the breasts of a pheasant, for example, then skinning is an easier and certainly very much quicker option.

Skinning

There is very little to save on the wings of any game bird, so it is probably easiest just to cut them straight off the bird at the joint where the wing-bone joins the body. You can buy proper meat scissors that will cut through small ones but a pair of gardening secateurs works just as well. Remove the head and also the legs at the point where the scaly part joins the flesh and feathers. Next lay the bird on its back and, with a sharp-pointed knife, cut the skin gently along the direction of the breastbone, taking care not to cut into the flesh. It should then be possible to peel off the skin from the entire body – don't worry; you'll get better with each one you do! If you are just after the breast meat, you only need to peel back sufficient skin to allow access and then cut down each side of the breastbone, making sure that the point of the knife cuts as close to the bones as possible. You should end up with two escalopes.

Plucking

Big birds such as geese could be plucked whilst the carcass is suspended by its legs from a rafter in a shed, but for others, it is perhaps easier to sit on a box and position the bird comfortably across both knees. It will pay to cover yourself with a sack or, better still, wear overalls, as the fine downy feathers of any bird are quite good at attaching themselves to woollen jumpers, human hair and in finding their way down your Wellingtons!

Begin by pulling out the main wing feathers and then, with the bird on its back and its head facing away from you, hold the skin tight with one hand and pull out the breast feathers slowly and gently (towards the head) with the other hand. Game birds such as partridge or pheasant have a more delicate skin than, say, a mallard, and you will no doubt tear it a few times until you get the hang of it. Slowly remove all the feathers from the breast, legs and under-wing area before turning the bird over and completing the wings and back.

If the bird was freshly killed, any stubbly feathers can be removed once the bird has cooled and the skin has begun to set firm. To finish the job, singe off the body hairs with a cigarette lighter, lighted taper or over a gas flame.

Evisceration

Cut off the head at the top of the neck and loosen the skin there until it is possible to pull out the windpipe and crop before cutting off the neck close to the body, leaving just a flap of skin. With the point of a sharp knife, cut around the vent and remove it. Now comes the bit not for the faint-hearted! Holding the bird steady with one hand, push two fingers of the other into the vent area and feel for the intestines – by pushing right up into the breast cavity, it should be possible to pull out everything all in one movement.

As a good chef, you should retain the heart, liver and gizzard, the latter of which should be split open and cleaned. Discard the rest of the guts. The offal saved (including the neck) can then be used for making stock. If you think you are likely to get sufficient over the season, you could freeze the livers until you have enough to make pâté.

Snipe and woodcock are not usually eviscerated, but the gizzard should be removed via a small cut made in the side of the body. Traditionally, the head should be skinned and left attached to the carcass, but it is not for the squeamish and, unless you are intending to follow the old French practice of re-heating the head over a candle and eating it at the end of the meat course, there are no benefits in doing so.

HARES AND RABBITS

A rabbit will have had its intestines removed (paunched) as soon as it has been killed; a hare may have been left to hang with its intestines intact. Other than this fact, they are skinned in much the same way.

Cut around each leg and slit the skin down their length. For hares, nick the belly fur and cut along the length of the underbelly, taking care not to break through the skin and into the paunch (the belly skin of a rabbit will already have been cut due to the fact that it has previously been gutted). Loosen and pull away the skin from the back legs and, taking firm hold, pull the skin

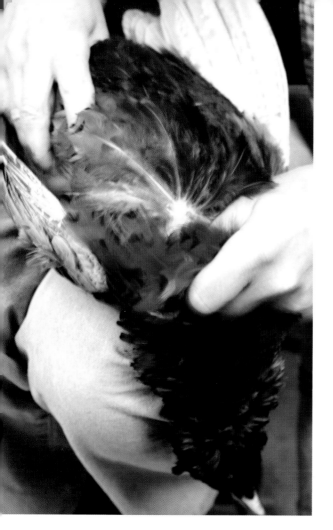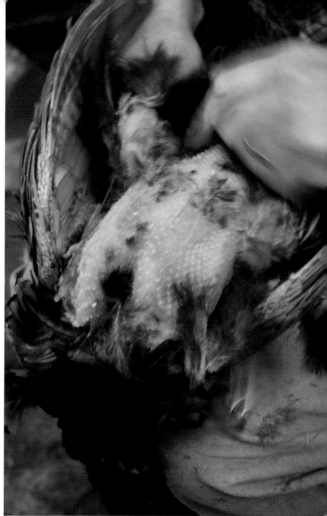

towards the head as if you were removing a pullover or dress. Cut off the head at the base of the neck (it should be attached to the skin if you've done the job properly) and remove the feet by cutting at the first leg joint.

Remove the guts of a hare by slitting the thin membrane of skin between the back legs and ribcage, but beware of piercing the contents as this will make the inside of the animal more difficult to clean.

Jointing

Cut off the legs by using a sharp knife to cut between the muscles that join the legs to the hips and shoulders, then cut through the bone at the joint with a strong knife – if you can pinpoint the exact place where the bone joint is, it is a very easy procedure. The saddle can be cut into even portions depending on the size of the animal (expect to get two or three or maybe four from a hare). Again, the saddle is easiest jointed by inserting a knife between the vertebrae rather than trying to hack through randomly. If you intend doing much jointing and preparation, it may pay to invest in a butcher's cleaver as, with that, you can chop through at almost any point.

CLEANING AND GUTTING FISH

Use a very sharp knife and insert the point into the hole (vent) at the tail end of the belly. Slit the belly open by cutting towards the head end in much the same way as you would use a paper knife to open an envelope, taking care not to rip into the intestines. Once this has been done, tip the insides out and use your fingers (or a spoon if you're the slightest bit squeamish) and scrape away anything still remaining, taking particular care to remove the transparent 'skin' that runs along the backbone. Make sure that any blood is thoroughly washed away, otherwise there is a good chance that it might spoil the taste of the fish once cooked.

Descaling

Trout and salmon do not need descaling, but with other types that are presented on the plate intact, and which have large scales (pike, for example), they should be descaled by holding the fish firmly at the tail end (dipping your fingers in salt will give a better grip) and running the back of a knife several times from tail to head.

Skinning an Eel

Not without good reason has the expression 'as slippery as an eel' arisen – fresh eels are pretty difficult to skin and possible the best way of doing so is to cut the skin right around the neck before making a slit the whole length. Hammer a strong nail at a convenient height (not in the kitchen, obviously!) and push the eel's jaws onto it so that it is firmly impaled (you could use a butcher's hook). Hold the head end of the skin – you will gain a better grip if you hold it with a tea towel or similar cloth – and pull the skin off sharply in much the same way as trying to create maximum pain by ripping off a sticking plaster from a hairy leg or arm!

TIP

A useful tip for anyone handling game, fish, rabbits or poultry, is to add half a teaspoon of ordinary mustard powder to the soap lather on your hands when washing them.

HYGIENE IN PREPARATION

If working in a shed, barn or garage and the proposed work surfaces are unlikely to be of the cleanest order, spread a piece of heavy-duty plastic sheet out and work on that.

Any work surfaces should be meticulously cleaned both before and after eviscerating game or jointing animals such as boar or deer. Dettol spray is an excellent anti-bacterial surface cleaner, which, although effective at killing germs, does not, however, contain bleach and will not taint or smell. Secateurs, knives, butcher's saws and the like need special treatment and, where it is possible to do so, they should be stripped down so that every niche is thoroughly scrubbed and washed before being given the Dettol treatment.

STOCKING THE FREEZER

Laziness may tempt you into freezing game whilst still in the fur or feather – don't – it is bad practice and the meat will suffer due to air being trapped under the feathers or between the fur.

It is important to have an organized freezer where everything is instantly accessible. An untidy heap of badly labelled and poorly stored joints and a mixed variety of game can result in those at the very bottom never getting used and eventually being thrown away due to becoming 'out-of-date' or succumbing to the effects of freezer burn. Game kept too long, whilst remaining useable, certainly tends to lose some of its flavour and none should be kept frozen for more than twelve months at the very outside. Always keep a record of what goes in and what comes out, preferably on a wipe-clean board fixed close to where the freezer is kept.

A chest freezer is often best, provided that it contains sufficient trays to accommodate all of a specific game species – it is then a simple matter to lift out the other trays until one accesses the particular one being sought, 'Pheasant', for example. One tray should be kept for odd joints and perhaps labelled 'Mixed Bag' or something similar and will contain that odd brace of grouse given by a friend on their return from North Yorkshire, a hare, those ostrich steaks bought on a whim at the local agricultural show and the eel that someone gave you, but you've yet to decide how best to deal with.

Within each tray, try and ensure that the oldest labelled bags are placed to the top so that their contents are always the first to be used and ensure that any sharp or protruding bones do not puncture the bag in which they are wrapped by wrapping them in kitchen foil. It is also important to make sure that all air is excluded from the bag by the simple expedient of inserting a drinking straw into the almost closed neck of the polythene bag and sucking it out.

Remember that a full freezer operates far more efficiently than one that is only partially full. With careful stacking, the space between the trays and their contents is much reduced. If necessary, fill any gaps in the freezer with newspapers.

ROASTING TIPS

The purpose of this particular recipe book is to show the exciting and imaginative alternatives to the traditional method of roasting game. However, there are occasions when a roast is desired and so it is only right that a few general tips should be included.

By its very nature, game is a lean, non-fatty meat and to ensure that a roasting bird or joint does not dry out during its time in the oven, it is necessary to cook it slowly after adding extra 'moisture'. This can be done prior to cooking with the aid of a marinade (*see* Chapter 15) or adding it to the bird or joint immediately before roasting.

In the 'old days', when the consumption of butter and the like was not considered too great a problem, it was usual to put butter both inside and outside the bird and, as an added precaution, cover it with strips of bacon. A more acceptable alternative nowadays would be to use olive oil in

A ROASTING GUIDE

A very rough guide to roasting times for the most commonly available roasts is as follows. Note, however, that specific recipes may detail different timings.

- Grouse – gas mark 5, 190°C/375°F for 30–40min.
- Partridge: for 20–25min.
- Pheasant: for 45–60min.
- Guinea-Fowl: for 45–60min.
- Quail: for 15min.
- Woodcock: for 20min.
- Venison: for 30 minutes per 450g/1lb (but *refer* to the beginning of Chapter 8 for more detailed information)
- Pigeon: gas mark 6, 200°C/400°F for 20–30min.
- Mallard: for 30–35min.
- Teal: for 15–20min.
- Saddle of hare: for 35min.
- Whole rabbit: for 45–60min.
- Snipe: gas mark 7, 220°C/425°F for 10min.
- Wild goose: for 15min per 450g/1b.

NB Venison can be cooked at gas mark 8, 230°C/450°F for 10–15 minutes per 450g/1lb if desired to be served pink or at gas mark ¼, 100°C/225°F for 45 minutes per 450g/1lb, plus 45 minutes, if required well done.

place of butter. It also helps to moisten game by inserting a peeled apple, sliced orange or onion into the body cavity and basting frequently.

To avoid the necessity for basting, you could try wrapping the bird or joint in kitchen foil and, halfway through the cooking time, turn the meat over and once again seal the foil 'envelope'. Open and fold back the foil when roasting is almost complete in order to give the meat an attractive crisp and brown appearance.

BARBECUING GAME AND FISH

Game-bird breasts, certain fish and even the haunches of young grey squirrels can be successfully barbecued, as can the breasts of pigeon when 'butterflied' – slit almost in half with a knife, then opened out and gently flattened. You could also try the same with the breasts of young rooks, but they are perhaps best cooked in the traditional rook pie or as part of a casserole. Ostrich steaks, small venison and wild boar joints also make for an unusual barbecue that is so much more interesting than the conventional beefsteak and sausages. Try the 'bunny burgers', made famous by Hugh Fearnley-Whittingstall – as with all forms of cooking, all it takes is imagination and experimentation.

One of the best ways of adding flavour to game intended to be barbecued or wood grilled is simply to rub it with freshly crushed cloves of garlic, and sprinkle it with lemon juice and herbs such as rosemary, thyme or fennel before finally brushing it with olive oil and giving it a light sprinkling of sea salt just before the meat or fish to be cooked is put over the heat.

CHOPPING ONIONS

Life, as was once famously claimed, is too short to stuff a mushroom – much the same applies to chopping onions and, as this particular vegetable features in many recipes, marinades and helpful hints, it seems sensible to describe a quick method of chopping and/or dicing.

Stand an onion on its base (the point to which the roots have been growing!) and cut several slices almost to the bottom in one direction. Turn it and cut a second series of slices across the first, before setting the onion on its side and slicing across all of the previous cuts. Voila! Perfectly and evenly chopped onion – obviously the closer the slices to one another, the more finely chopped it will be.

As for that other perennial problem of chopping onions – that of their juices making you cry – traditional remedies range from the sublime to the bizarre and include slicing whilst holding a spoon in your mouth, and preparing an onion with it, and your hands, underwater (a potentially dangerous operation and definitely not one to be recommended). By far the easiest is to grin and bear it – smile through the tears, in fact!

CASSEROLES

Some game or joints of game are best served as a casserole, either because of their age or the fact that the type of meat benefits from a long, slow method of cooking in order to realize its full potential. Rabbit, for instance, has a tendency towards dryness and it is advisable to either stew or casserole for this reason. Certain joints of venison can be very dry and taste infinitely better when belly pork or *lardons* have been added and all have been placed into a heavy oven-proof dish together with home-made stock (*see* Chapter 15), vegetables such as carrots and onions or shallots and plenty of flavour-some herbs as are recommended for barbecuing.

A casserole or stew is also a good way of using up odd pieces of meat left over from butchering and jointing, but it is important to realize that when including different types of meat in the one dish, some may cook quicker than others and a long cooking time with a low oven temperature is the best way of ensuring that all are equally tender.

Glossary

Albumen – Egg white.

Al dente – Vegetables or, more commonly, pasta, cooked, but firm to the bite.

Allumette – Vegetables, potatoes or other items cut into the size and shape of matchsticks.

Arroser – To sprinkle with liquid or to baste.

Bain marie – A deep container; half-filled with water in which other cooking pots are placed in order to cook gently in the oven. Usually used for terrines and similar dishes.

Bard – Place slices of bacon over the breast of game to prevent it from drying out when roasting.

Basting – Regularly spooning over the meat some of the fat or liquid in which it is cooking.

Beurre manié – A mixture, by equal parts of flour and butter, used to thicken sauces. *See also* Roux.

Bouillon – Un-clarified stock or broth from meat or fish.

Bouquet garni – Sprig of thyme, parsley and bay leaf, tied together and used to flavour stews and casseroles.

Braising – A combination of roasting and stewing; usually used on tougher joints of meat.

Cassoulet – A casserole of stewed meat and beans.

Cayenne – Powdered red pepper.

Clarified butter – Butter cleared of impurities by melting slowly and removing the unwanted liquid that forms at the base.

Croûton – Small cube of fried or toasted bread served as a garnish to soup or alongside certain game dishes.

De-glaze – To loosen meat residue in a pan or roasting dish, after roasting or frying, with a wooden spoon and add wine or stock in order to make gravy.

Duxelle – A purée of very finely chopped mushrooms, sweated in butter, with a little chopped onion, which can then be used for stuffing game birds or as a sauce base.

Earthenware – Cooking pot made of fired clay.

Entrecôte – Boned steak.

Etouffé – A cooking method similar to braising in which items are cooked with little or no added liquid in a pan with a tight-fitting lid.

Farina – Flour or meal made of cereal, nuts, or starchy roots.

Farrago – Medley or mixture of foodstuffs.

Filo (pastry) – A type of leaved pastry.

Fumet – Liquid in which fish has been cooked, or the juices that have run from meat during cooking.

Garnish – To decorate food dishes, especially just before serving.

Gazpacho – Soup served cold – the name originating from Spain.

Gelatine – Transparent tasteless substance used to bind or fix ingredients in certain dishes.

Haslet – Pieces of offal cooked together, usually as a meat loaf.

Infuse – Steep herbs or similar in liquid in order to extract the flavoursome content.

Isinglass – Gelatine obtained from fish, especially sturgeon, and used in solidifying the contents of certain dishes. Also a traditional ingredient used in preserving eggs.

Julienne – Vegetables cut into short thin strips.

Larding – A method whereby thin strips of fat are pushed through meat in order to prevent it from drying out during cooking.

Lardons – Small squares of bacon or pork belly-fat.

Marinade – To marinate meat or fish is to leave it soaking for several hours in a combination of oils, wine and herbs (*see* Chapter 15).

Medallions – Small rounds of meat.

Papillote – Greaseproof paper or kitchen foil forming a casing around food in order that, in the case of fish, for example, it can steam, or, in the case of meat, self-baste whilst roasting.

Ragout – Meat stewed with vegetables and highly seasoned.

Reducing – Boiling a liquid such as that in which fish and game has been cooked, in order that the taste is concentrated and makes a base for sauces or gravy.

Roulade – Rolled piece of meat, fish or pastry into which a filling has been added.

Roux – A mixture of fat and flour used in sauces.

Quenelles – Technically, a lightly poached dumpling based on a mixture or combination of chicken, veal, game or fish, bound with eggs and shaped into an oval by the use of two spoons, but used generally to describe the method of serving mashed potatoes and/or vegetables.

Sauté – Rapid cooking in oil, usually in a heavy-bottomed sauce or frying pan.

Searing – To quickly brown meat at a high temperature in order to retain its juices.

Spatchcock – Opening a bird by cutting through its breastbone and flattening – usually, but not always, associated with pan-frying.

Sweat – Cooking vegetables very slowly in butter or oil so as to draw out the moisture and soften them. Care must be taken that the fat does not become too hot and brown otherwise the vegetables will just remain raw and burn.

Trivet – A metal rack placed over or in a roasting tin to keep the meat from sitting in its own juices.

Trussing – A method of holding game or meat together by tying with string and the aid of a skewer.

Whisk – Utensil for whisking or the action of whipping or mixing eggs, cream and so on, with a brisk sweeping movement. Usually necessary in recipes where air needs to be added, such as in the making of soufflés.

Wine vinegar – Vinegar made from wine as opposed to malt and so on.

Wood grilling – By barbecuing over charcoal, the wood imparts a distinctive and unique flavour to the meat.

Zest – Scraping of orange, lemon or lime peel used as flavouring.

'At-a-Glance' Recipe List

The enclosed list is as they appear in the text: to see them grouped in alphabetical order, together with more detailed references from chapter to chapter, please refer to the Index.

Chilled Pheasant and Apple Soup
Fruity 'Not-Quite-There' Pheasant
    Curry
Chestnut and Orange Pheasant
    Casserole
Thai Green Pheasant
Spanish Pheasant and Chestnut
    Autumn Stew
French Pheasant with Country
    Topping
Pan-Fried Pheasant Breasts in
    Bacon
Fruity, Nutty Pheasant
Orchard and Onion Pheasant
Braised Pheasant in Calvados,
    Elderflower and Pineapple
Roast Pheasant
Roast Pheasant with Madeira
Tea-Leaf Smoked Pheasant Breasts
Pheasant Pâté
Pheasant Enchiladas
Pheasant and Roast Pepper Pasta
Pheasant and Pancetta Rolls
Pheasant and Endive Salad
Partridge and Pea Risotto Soup
Sherried Cream Partridge Livers
Partridge Pot-Roast
Simple Poached Partridge
Partridge, Pimms and Plums
Partridge and Kumquat Casserole
Partridge, the Italian Way
Partridge Risotto
Partridge in Tarragon Sauce
Partridge Cutlets
Partridge Breasts with Oyster
    Mushrooms and Chanterelles
Partridges in their Nest
Classic Roast Grouse
Casserole of Grouse
Scottish Grouse and Haggis
    Stuffing

Truffled Grouse
Grouse Soup
Grouse Breasts in Cream
Grouse, Grapes and Grappa
Grouse Terrine
Simple Snipe Bites
Roast Snipe or Woodcock
Snipe on a Skewer
Regency Woodcock
Woodcock Breasts in Cognac
Woodcock Perigordine
Grouse, Snipe and Woodcock
    Melange
Roast Mallard
Mallard Breasts with Blueberry,
    Orange and Mint Salsa
Rhubarb Duck and Ginger
Teal with Roasted Salsify and
    Sweetcorn Purée
Spit-Roasted Wild Duck
Pan-Fried Saba Duck with
    Horseradish Celeriac Rôstis
Teal with Cider and Apples
Pot-Roasted Widgeon
Duck Breast Salad with Raspberry
    Dressing
Duck Timbales
Stuffed Goose Breast
Crispy Goose Tex-Mex Casserole
Roast Goose
Wild Goose Stew
Goose Provençale
Young Wild Goose with Potato
    Stuffing
Grilled Pigeon
Braised Pigeon with Orange
Pigeon Pâté
Quick and Easy Pigeon Cannelloni
Pigeon in Minutes
Pigeon Breasts in a Wild Mushroom
    Sauce

Pigeon with Warmed Mushroom
    Salad
Pigeon with Tomato and Chocolate
    Sauce
Petit Pigeon Puddings
Pigeon 'Scampi'
Pigeon Almondine
Boiled Pigeon
Hungarian Pigeon Soup with
    Picked Gherkins and Soured
    Cream
Stuffed Pigeon
Guinea-Fowl in Red Wine Sauce
Apple Creamed Guinea-Fowl with
    Morel Mushrooms
Guinea-Fowl in Caramelized
    Orange and Pink Peppercorn
    Sauce
Sautéed Guinea-Fowl and Cabbage
Russian Guinea-Fowl
Creole Guinea-Fowl with Pineapple
Caille Papillons
Caille al la Crapaudine
Caille Rôsti
Cailles en Cocotte (casseroled
    quail)
Pan-Cooked Quail with Olives
Roast Quail with Noodles
Quail Richelieu
Quail Tagine
Potted Quail Eggs with Anchovy
Curried Quail Eggs
Scrambled Quail Eggs and Truffle
Paella Valenciana with Rabbit
Rabbit in White Wine and Mustard
Lapin en Cidre
Rabbit and Prunes
Devilled Rabbit
Steam Stuffed Saddle of Rabbit
    with Nettle Mash
Curried Rabbit

Rabbit Salmerejo
Terrine of Hare
Hare Pâté
Creamed Saddle of Hare
Hare in a Sweet and Sour Sauce
Hare and Dumplings
Landlord's Hare
Italian Hare
Venison Liver
Deer Kidneys in a Batter Bed
Creamed Venison Sweetbreads
Venison and Wild Mushrooms
Venison with Fresh Pear Chutney
Parsley-Breaded Rack of Venison
    with a Blackcurrant Sauce
Parcelled Venison Steak
Beer Curing (of boar hams)
Sweet Curing (of boar hams)
Curly Kale with Wild Boar
    Pancetta and Pecan Nuts
Braised Boar and Beetroot
Wild Boar Pancetta and Onion
    Ciabatta
Boar Chops Baked in Cream
Wild Boar Casserole with Beer
Cooked Boar Ham
Quiches and Tarts
Shortcrust Pastry
Flaky Pastry
Rough Puff Pastry
Hot-Water Crust Pastry
Cheese Pastry
Suet Pastry
Hob-Cooked Hot Game Pie
Puff Pastry
Game Suet Pudding
Mini Game Pie Surprises
Raised Game Pie
Perfect Pigeon Pie
Venison Sausage Pie
Rook Pie
Rabbit Pie
Pheasant Weaves
Rabbit and Macaroni Pie
Rabbit and Venison Sausage
    Crumble
Simple Fish Pie
Fish Quiche
Fish Loaves
Salmon Loaf
Easy, Herby Trout
Trout Pasta Pots
Trout in Oatmeal
Smoked Trout Soufflé
Smoked Salmon and Trout Terrine
Simple Salmon and Samphire
Salmon Steaks and Fennel

Carpaccio of Salmon
Spinach and Salmon Lasagne
Pike Steaks, Loire-style
Baked Zander Pie
Zander with White Butter
Carp Stuffed with Caviar and
    Capers
Baked Perch in White Wine
Larded Pike
Boiled Pike with Oysters
Eels Marinara
Buttered Eels
Smoked Salmon Fishcakes
Trout Marsala
Trout and Bacon Parcels
Pigeon Fajitas
Pigeon and Cranberry Crostini
Crispy Pheasant Rolls
Pheasant Tetrazzini
Pheasant Wrap
Venison and Onion Marmalade
    Steaks
Deerstalker's Pie
Venison Sausage and Apple
    Kebabs
Drambuie-Soaked Venison Kebabs
Dooh! Ducknuts!
Duck Quenelles with Noodles
Game Fondue
Kangaroo Pizza Wedges
Ostrich Burgers with Balsamic and
    Tomato Relish
Buffalo Steak Sandwich
Faison de Chez Jacques
Country Pheasant Casserole
Pigeons with Cherries in Eau-de-
    Vie
Venison Casserole in Beer
Hand-Raised Grouse and Foie Gras
    Pie with Apricots and Wild
    Mushrooms
Jugged Hare in Chocolate
Goose and/or Pigeon Stir-Fry
Salmon Stuffed with Crab and
    Spinach with Dill Sauce
Pheasant – Baden-Style
Salmagundi
Gamekeeper's Tandoori
Young Pheasants in Parcels
The Lady Friend's Pike Pie
Grilled Partridge wiith Garlic, Oil,
    Lemon and Cayenne
Crocodile Tail Steak Fillet
Kangaroo with Kiwi, Cashew Nuts
    and Dates
Kangaroo with Mango and
    Coconut

Ostrich Steaks with Nutmeg
    Creamed Spinach
Ostrich and Date Brochette in a
    Spicy Marinade
Rook Lyonnaise
Squirrel and Dumplings
Squirrel Fricassee
Wild Herb Vinegar
Pears Filled with Hazelnut and
    Cheese-Balls
Blackberry Dressing
Pear and Mint Jelly
Crab Apple Chutney
Classic Sloe Gin
Shooter's Punch
Parsnip and Apple Mash
Turnip and Tarragon Rôsti
Parsnips in Batter
Bubble and Squeak
Spring Onion Potato Cakes
French Mix Vegetables
Game Chips
Bread Dumplings
Mushroom Dumplings
Cranberry Stuffing
Apple and Herb Stuffing
Chestnut Stuffing
Spinach and Mushroom Stuffing
Lemon and Mushroom Stuffing
Classic Green Salad
Rice and Orange Salad
Risotto with Fresh Asparagus and
    Mushrooms
Garnish of Young Turnip Leaves
Green Mayonnaise
Ginger and Garlic Marinade
Hollandaise Sauce
Cream or White Sauce
Brown Sauce
Sweet Sauce
Creamed Apple Sauce
Raisin Sauce
Staffordshire Venison Sauce
Sauce Rouenaise
Marsala Sauce
Onion and Lemon Sauce
Lemon Sauce
Aromatic Sauce
Cucumber Cream Sauce
Figaro Sauce
Samphire Sauce
Picada
Jellied Stock
Brown Stock
Fish Stock
Game Stock
Giblet Stock

Index